COMMUNICATION ENGLISH 2

SECOND EDITION

KMU CE Committee

Keimyung University Press

Communication English 2nd Edition Book 2

KMU CE Committee

Project Editor: Casey Malarcher / **Acquisitions Editor:** Matthew Broadhurst, Tamara Gaskill / **Content Editor:** Peggy Anderson, Andrea Janzen
Illustrator: Julia Filipone Erez / **Cover/Interior Design:** Design Plus, designssoul

ISBN: 978-89-7585-807-9

11 10 9 8 7 6 5 4 3
21 20

Photo Credits
All images © Shutterstock, Inc. except: p. 99 © Photos.com

Printed in Korea

CONTENTS

Map of the Book

Unit	Title	Talking About
01	Daily Life	Things we do every day
02	Giving Directions	How to give directions to people
03	Sickness & Health	Being healthy and getting sick
04	Cooking	Describing foods and how to cook them
05	Around the World	Different cultures and countries
06	Telling Stories	Things that have happened to us
07	Eating Out	Eating at a restaurant
08	Unreal Situations	Imagined events
09	Future Plans	Things that haven't happened yet
10	The Korean Push for English Education	Importance of English to Koreans
11	The Westernization of Korean Society	Examples of the Westernization of Korea
12	A Developed Korea	How Korea has changed

Classroom Language

01	Can I ask (you) a question?	질문해도 될까요?
02	Could you repeat the instructions, please?	어떻게 하는지 한 번 더 설명해주시겠어요?
03	What is our homework?	숙제가 뭐예요?
04	How do you say that word?	그 단어를 어떻게 말하나요?
05	How do you say "사전" in English?	"사전"을 영어로 어떻게 말하나요?
06	I don't know how to say it in English.	영어로 어떻게 말하는지 모르겠어요.
07	I'm sorry Mr./Mrs./Miss/Ms. A, I didn't bring my English book.	A 선생님 죄송하지만, 영어책을 안 갖고 왔어요.
08	It's at home.	집에 있습니다.
09	Did you have a good weekend?	주말 잘 보냈나요?
10	I'm sorry I'm late.	늦어서 죄송합니다.
11	When is this due?	언제까지인가요?
12	Can I ask someone in Korean?	한국어로 질문해도 될까요?
13	Do you mind if I speak Korean?	한국어를 사용해도 될까요?
14	How do you spell "A"?	"A"의 철자는 무엇인가요?
15	We're finished.	끝났습니다.
16	What do we do next?	다음에는 무엇을 하나요?
17	Could I be excused?	빠져도 될까요? / 화장실에 가도 될까요?

How to Use Units 01-09

Communication English has been carefully structured to gradually introduce students to new topics, teaching them new vocabulary, grammar, and expressions until they are comfortable with speaking to a partner or to the class. Find out how each page works, and get ready to talk a lot!

PAGE 1

Warm-Up uses a large photograph and simple activities to ease students into the new unit.

Model Dialog is a natural conversation designed to introduce the unit's vocabulary and grammar.

UNIT 01 Daily Life

Warm-Up
What time do you wake up on weekdays?
Do you normally eat breakfast in the morning?

Talking About:
Things we do every day

1 Model Dialog

Listen and practice the dialog with a partner. Track 1

Veronica: Patrick, you look tired today. What time did you go to bed last night?
Patrick: Hi Veronica, what's up? Yeah, I'm pretty sleepy. I got to bed around 3:00 a.m.
Veronica: Three in the morning? Wow, that's late. Did you go out last night?
Patrick: No, I was studying for this big test next week.
Veronica: Oh, so you were up all night studying? That's too bad.
Patrick: Yeah, I was drinking coffee and energy drinks to stay awake.
Veronica: Oh, my. That's not good for you, you know. Coffee makes me sick.
Patrick: Yeah, I regret it now. I missed my first class this morning, actually!
Veronica: I always set my alarm for 7:00 a.m. so I can get to class early.
Patrick: Well, you're a better student than me!

Speaking Success!

There are many ways of **greeting** people in casual speech. They are posed as questions, but are often used simply as a substitute for "hello."

What's up?
How's it going?
How are things?

Talking About introduces students to the focus of the current unit.

Speaking Success! teaches elements of everyday spoken English to improve students' understanding and fluency.

PAGE 2

Vocabulary introduces key vocabulary for the unit, and activities encourage students to use these words right away.

Essential Expressions features key vocabulary that will be useful in the rest of the unit.

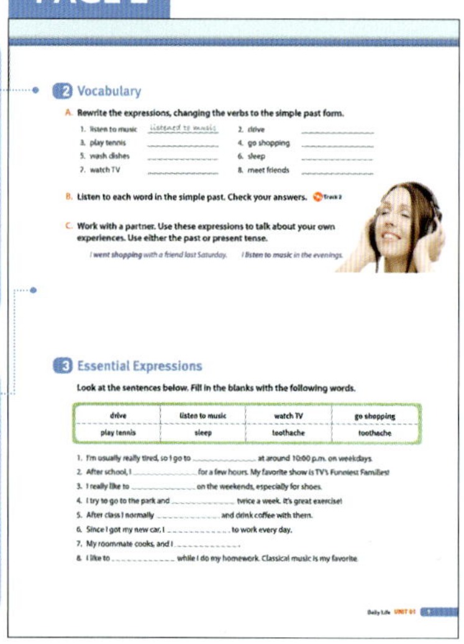

2 Vocabulary

A. Rewrite the expressions, changing the verbs to the simple past form.

1. listen to music *listened to music* 2. drive ______
3. play tennis ______ 4. go shopping ______
5. wash dishes ______ 6. sleep ______
7. watch TV ______ 8. meet friends ______

B. Listen to each word in the simple past. Check your answers. Track 2

C. Work with a partner. Use these expressions to talk about your own experiences. Use either the past or present tense.

I went shopping with a friend last Saturday. *I listen to music in the evenings.*

3 Essential Expressions

Look at the sentences below. Fill in the blanks with the following words.

drive	listen to music	watch TV	go shopping
play tennis	sleep	toothache	toothache

1. I'm usually really tired, so I go to ______ at around 10:00 p.m. on weekdays.
2. After school, I ______ for a few hours. My favorite show is TV's Funniest Families!
3. I really like to ______ on the weekends, especially for shoes.
4. I try to go to the park and ______ twice a week. It's great exercise!
5. After class I normally ______ and drink coffee with them.
6. Since I got my new car, I ______ to work every day.
7. My roommate cooks, and I ______.
8. I like to ______ while I do my homework. Classical music is my favorite.

Daily Life UNIT 01 7

PAGE 3

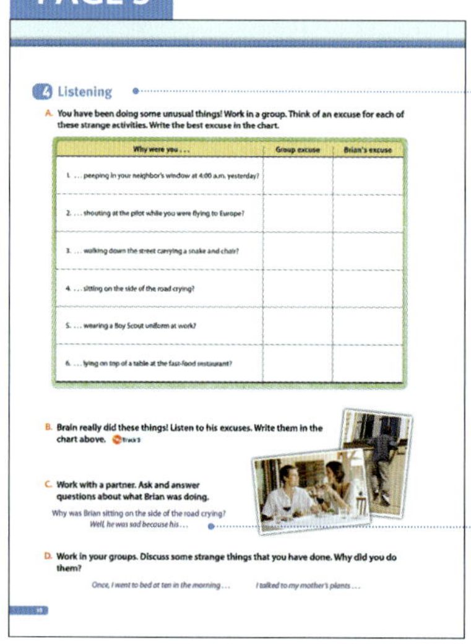

4 Listening

A. You have been doing some unusual things! Work in a group. Think of an excuse for each of these strange activities. Write the best excuse in the chart.

Why were you . . .	Group excuse	Brian's excuse
1. . . . peeping in your neighbor's window at 4:00 a.m. yesterday?		
2. . . . shouting at the pilot while you were flying to Europe?		
3. . . . walking down the street carrying a snake and chair?		
4. . . . sitting on the side of the road crying?		
5. . . . wearing a Boy Scout uniform at work?		
6. . . . lying on top of a table at the fast-food restaurant?		

B. Brain really did these things! Listen to his excuses. Write them in the chart above. Track 3

C. Work with a partner. Ask and answer questions about what Brian was doing.

Why was Brian sitting on the side of the road crying?
Well, he was sad because his . . .

D. Work in your groups. Discuss some strange things that you have done. Why did you do them?

Once, I went to bed at ten in the morning . . . *I talked to my mother's plants . . .*

Listening features native speakers talking about themselves, allowing students to improve their listening comprehension skills.

To build fluency and confidence, example responses are provided with speaking activities.

Interview/Survey sections begin to introduce speaking more prominently, encouraging students to speak to other members of their class.

Students are asked to write down what they learn from speaking to their classmates.

Students are encouraged to work together to talk about what they have learned.

PAGE 4

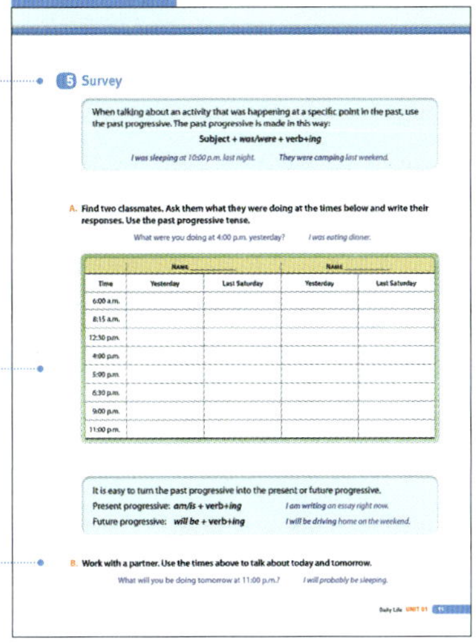

5 Survey

When talking about an activity that was happening at a specific point in the past, use the past progressive. The past progressive is made in this way:

Subject + was/were + verb+ing

I was sleeping at 10:00 p.m. last night. *They were camping last weekend.*

A. Find two classmates. Ask them what they were doing at the times below and write their responses. Use the past progressive tense.

What were you doing at 4:00 p.m. yesterday? *I was eating dinner.*

	Name ______		Name ______	
Time	Yesterday	Last Saturday	Yesterday	Last Saturday
6:00 a.m.				
8:15 a.m.				
12:30 p.m.				
4:00 p.m.				
5:00 p.m.				
6:30 p.m.				
9:00 p.m.				
11:00 p.m.				

It is easy to turn the past progressive into the present or future progressive.

Present progressive: *am/is* + verb+*ing* — *I am writing on essay right now.*

Future progressive: *will be* + verb+*ing* — *I will be driving home on the weekend.*

B. Work with a partner. Use the times above to talk about today and tomorrow.

What will you be doing tomorrow at 11:00 p.m.? *I will probably be sleeping.*

Daily Life UNIT 01

PAGE 5

6 Partner-Up

A. Work with a partner. Partner A looks at this page, and Partner B looks at page 87. Tell your partner what you did yesterday. Use the simple past tense.

I woke up at 9:00. Then I checked my email. After that I . . .

Partner A

Grammar Tip

Use **sequence markers** to show the order in which something happened.

First . . . Then . . . After that . . . Next . . . Afterwards . . . Later . . . Finally . . .

B. Close your book. Try to remember what your partner did yesterday.

C. Work with your partner. Talk about what you will do tomorrow. Use the future progressive tense.

Tomorrow I will be waking up at around 7:00 a.m., as usual! I will be eating a boiled egg for breakfast at . . .

Partner-Up asks students to work with a partner in a range of speaking activities.

Working with a partner helps to improve students' speaking and confidence levels.

PAGE 6

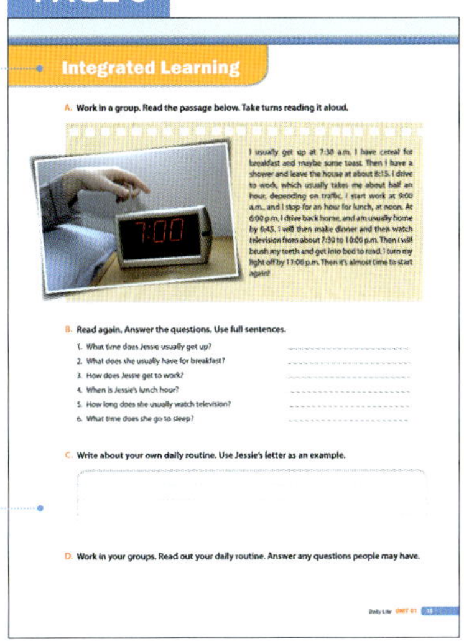

Integrated Learning

A. Work in a group. Read the passage below. Take turns reading it aloud.

I usually get up at 7:30 a.m. I have cereal for breakfast and maybe some toast. Then I have a shower and leave the house at about 8:15. I drive to work, which usually takes me about half an hour, depending on traffic. I start work at 9:00 a.m., and I stop for an hour for lunch, at noon. At 6:00 p.m. I drive back home, and am usually home by 6:45. I will then make dinner and then watch television from about 7:30 to 10:00 p.m. Then I will brush my teeth and get into bed to read. I turn my light off by 11:00 p.m. Then it's almost time to start again!

B. Read again. Answer the questions. Use full sentences.

1. What time does Jessie usually get up?
2. What does she usually have for breakfast?
3. How does Jessie get to work?
4. When is Jessie's lunch hour?
5. How long does she usually watch television?
6. What time does she go to sleep?

C. Write about your own daily routine. Use Jessie's letter as an example.

D. Work in your groups. Read out your daily routine. Answer any questions people may have.

Daily Life UNIT 01

Integrated Learning concludes each unit, checking and expanding upon the skills learned throughout the unit.

More key skills are called upon, featuring reading and writing in addition to listening and speaking.

UNIT 01 Daily Life

Warm-Up

What time do you wake up on weekdays?
Do you normally eat breakfast in the morning?

Talking About:
Things we do every day

1 Model Dialog

Listen and practice the dialog with a partner. Track 1

Veronica: Patrick, you look tired today. What time did you go to bed last night?

Patrick: Hi Veronica, what's up? Yeah, I'm pretty sleepy. I got to bed around 3:00 a.m.

Veronica: Three in the morning? Wow, that's late. Did you go out last night?

Patrick: No, I was studying for this big test next week.

Veronica: Oh, so you were up all night studying? That's too bad.

Patrick: Yeah, I was drinking coffee and energy drinks to stay awake.

Veronica: Oh, my. That's not good for you, you know. Coffee makes me sick.

Patrick: Yeah, I regret it now. I missed my first class this morning, actually!

Veronica: I always set my alarm for 7:00 a.m. so I can get to class early.

Patrick: Well, you're a better student than me!

Speaking Success!

There are many ways of **greeting** people in casual speech. They are posed as questions, but are often used simply as a substitute for "hello."

What's up?

How's it going?

How are things?

2 Vocabulary

A. Rewrite the expressions, changing the verbs to the simple past form.

1. listen to music ___listened to music___
2. drive ________________
3. play tennis ________________
4. go shopping ________________
5. wash dishes ________________
6. sleep ________________
7. watch TV ________________
8. meet friends ________________

B. Listen to each word in the simple past. Check your answers. Track 2

C. Work with a partner. Use these expressions to talk about your own experiences. Use either the past or present tense.

*I **went shopping** with a friend last Saturday.* *I **listen to music** in the evenings.*

3 Essential Expressions

Look at the sentences below. Fill in the blanks with the following words.

drive	listen to music	watch TV	go shopping
play tennis	~~sleep~~	meet friends	wash dishes

1. I'm usually really tired, so I go to ___sleep___ at around 10:00 p.m. on weekdays.
2. After school, I ________________ for a few hours. My favorite show is *TV's Funniest Families*!
3. I really like to ________________ at the mall on the weekends.
4. I usually ________________ at the park twice a week. It's great exercise!
5. After class I normally ________________ and drink coffee with them.
6. Since I got my new car, I ________________ to work every day.
7. My roommate cooks, and I ________________ after we eat.
8. I like to ________________ while I do my homework. Classical music is my favorite.

4 Listening

A. **You have been doing some unusual things! Work in a group. Think of an excuse for each of these strange activities. Write the best excuse in the chart.**

Why were you . . .	Group excuse	Brian's excuse
1. . . . peeping in your neighbor's window at 4:00 a.m. yesterday?		
2. . . . shouting at the pilot while you were flying to Europe?		
3. . . . walking down the street carrying a snake and chair?		
4. . . . sitting on the side of the road crying?		
5. . . . wearing a Boy Scout uniform at work?		
6. . . . lying on top of a table at the fast-food restaurant?		

B. **Brain really did these things! Listen to his excuses. Write them in the chart above.** Track 3

C. **Work with a partner. Ask and answer questions about what Brian was doing.**

Why was Brian sitting on the side of the road crying?

Well, he was sad because his . . .

D. **Work in your groups. Discuss some strange things that you have done. Why did you do them?**

Once, I went to bed at ten in the morning . . .

I talked to my mother's plants . . .

5 Survey

When talking about an activity that was happening at a specific point in the past, use the past progressive. The past progressive is made in this way:

Subject + *was/were* + verb+*ing*

***I was sleeping** at 10:00 p.m. last night.* ***They were camping** last weekend.*

A. Find two classmates. Ask them what they were doing at the times below and write their responses. Use the past progressive tense.

What were you doing at 4:00 p.m. yesterday? *I was eating dinner.*

	NAME ______		NAME ______	
Time	Yesterday	Last Saturday	Yesterday	Last Saturday
6:00 a.m.				
8:15 a.m.				
12:30 p.m.				
4:00 p.m.				
5:00 p.m.				
6:30 p.m.				
9:00 p.m.				
11:00 p.m.				

It is easy to turn the past progressive into the present or future progressive.

Present progressive: ***am/is* + verb+*ing*** ***I am writing** an essay right now.*

Future progressive: ***will be* + verb+*ing*** ***I will be driving** home on the weekend.*

B. Work with a partner. Use the times above to talk about today and tomorrow.

What will you be doing tomorrow at 11:00 p.m.? *I will probably be sleeping.*

6 Partner-Up

A. Work with a partner. Partner A looks at this page, and Partner B looks at page 124. Tell your partner what you did yesterday. Use the simple past tense.

I woke up at 9:00. Then I checked my email. After that I . . .

Partner A

After school

In the afternoon

After dinner

In the evening

Grammar Tip

Use **sequence markers** to show the order in which something happened.

First . . . *Then . . .* *After that . . .* *Next . . .* *Afterwards . . .* *Later . . .* *Finally . . .*

B. Close your book. Try to remember what your partner did yesterday.

C. Work with your partner. Talk about what you will do tomorrow. Use the future progressive tense.

Tomorrow I will be waking up at around 7:00 a.m., as usual! I will be eating a boiled egg for breakfast at . . .

Integrated Learning

1 Comprehension

A. Work in a group. Read the passage below. Take turns reading it aloud.

I usually get up at 7:30 a.m. I have cereal for breakfast and maybe some toast. Then I have a shower and leave the house at about 8:15. I drive to work, which usually takes me about half an hour, depending on traffic. I start work at 9:00 a.m., and I stop for an hour for lunch, at noon. At 6:00 p.m. I drive back home, and am usually home by 6:45. I will then make dinner and then watch television from about 7:30 to 10:00 p.m. Then I will brush my teeth and get into bed to read. I turn my light off by 11:00 p.m. Then it's almost time to start again!

B. Read again. Answer the questions. Use full sentences.

1. What time does Jessie usually get up? ______________________
2. What does she usually have for breakfast? ______________________
3. How does Jessie get to work? ______________________
4. When is Jessie's lunch hour? ______________________
5. How long does she usually watch television? ______________________
6. What time does she go to sleep? ______________________

C. Write about your own daily routine. Use Jessie's letter as an example.

____

____

____

D. Work in your groups. Read out your daily routine. Answer any questions people may have.

Practice

1 Dialog

A. Listen to the recording and write the missing words that you hear. Track 1

Veronica:	Patrick, you look tired ________. What time did you go to bed last night?
Patrick:	Hi, Veronica, what's up? Yeah, I'm ________ sleepy. I got to bed around **3:00** a.m.
Veronica:	**Three** in the ____________? Wow, that's late. Did you go out last night?
Patrick:	No, I was ______________ for this big test **next week**.
Veronica:	Oh, so you were up all night studying? That's too bad.
Patrick:	Yeah, I was drinking ______________ and **energy drinks** to stay awake.
Veronica:	Oh, my. That's not good for you, you know. Coffee makes me sick.
Patrick:	Yeah, I regret it now. I ___________ my first class this morning, actually!
Veronica:	I ____________ set my alarm for **7:00 a.m.** so I can get to class early.
Patrick:	Well, you're a better ____________ than me!

B. Look at the bolded words in the dialog above. With a partner, think of some new information to replace these words.

C. Practice the dialog using the new information.

2 Picture Description

Listen and choose the statement that best describes what you see in the picture. Track 4

1.

Ⓐ Ⓑ Ⓒ Ⓓ

2.

Ⓐ Ⓑ Ⓒ Ⓓ

3 Unscramble

Unscramble the sentences below.

1. time / now? / What / is it
   → What time is it now?

2. went to / My sister / class at / 9:30 a.m.
   → ______________________________

3. lunch / always eat / 1:00 p.m. / at around / I
   → ______________________________

4. movie theater / to the / at 7:30 p.m. / Last Tuesday / I went
   → ______________________________

5. Jane / in the / school choir / yesterday evening. / was singing
   → ______________________________

Note Taking

Main Points	Detail

Summary

Brainstorming

Journal/Activity Writing

UNIT 02 Giving Directions

Warm-Up

Do you ever ask for directions on the street?
Are you good at giving directions?

Talking About:
How to give directions to people

1 Model Dialog

Listen and practice the dialog with a partner. Track 5

Sara: Excuse me, sir. Could you help me, please? I'm a little lost.

Policeman: Of course. Where do you need to go, ma'am?

Sara: Well, I've been trying to find the Sea View Shopping Arcade for the last hour!

Policeman: OK. Let me help you. Go straight up this road until you reach the intersection.

Sara: Pardon me? I couldn't hear you.

Policeman: Walk up the road to the intersection. Then go straight until you see the bank.

Sara: Up the intersection, walk until I see the bank, right.

Policeman: Yep. The arcade is across from the bank. You can't miss it.

Sara: Thank you very much. You've been very helpful. I'm sure I'll find it now.

Policeman: My pleasure. Enjoy your shopping, ma'am.

Speaking Success!

If we do not hear or understand what someone has said, we can ask them to **repeat** themselves.

Pardon me?

Sorry?

(I beg your) pardon?

Excuse me?

2 Vocabulary

A. Look at the picture below. Complete the sentences with the correct prepositions of place.

in front of   behind   in   under   above   next to   on

1. The cat is ______________ the refrigerator.
2. The dog is ______________ the table.
3. The clock is ______________ the gas range.
4. The pet food is ______________ the cupboard.
5. The oven is ______________ the cat's bowl.
6. The bowl is ______________ the rice cooker.
7. The plant is ______________ the window.

B. Work with a partner. Look around the room. Make sentences using the words above.

*Jamie sits **behind** Lee.*   *My desk is **next to** the door.*

3 Essential Expressions

Look at the picture above. Fill in the blanks with the following words.

on	gas range	in front of	behind
next	table	cupboard	

1. The dog is under the kitchen ______________.
2. The knife is ______________ to the cake.
3. The clock is above the ______________.
4. The kettle is ______________ the gas range.
5. The cat's bowl is ______________ the oven.
6. The window is ______________ the plant.
7. The pet food is in the ______________.

4 Listening

A. **Look at the map and discuss it with a partner. Which places would you like to go to? Is it similar to your town?**

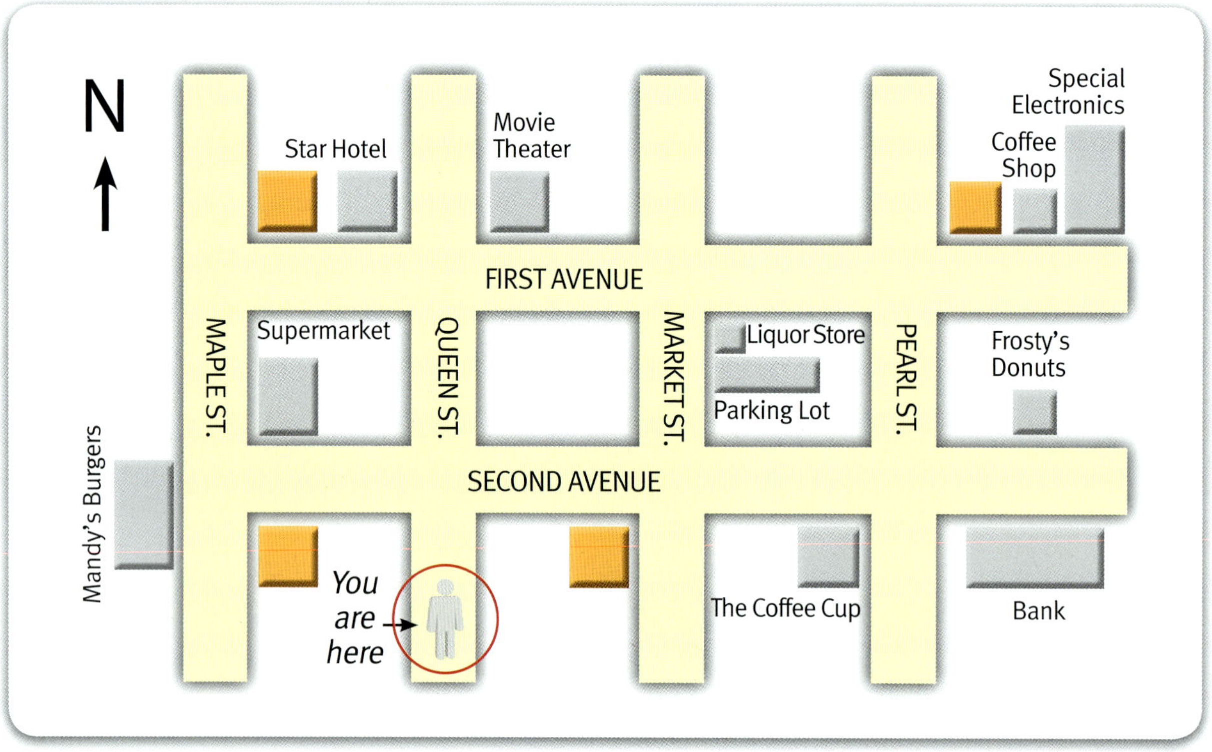

B. **Listen to the four people asking for directions. Starting from the same place every time, write the number of the dialog in the correct box on the map.** Track 6

C. **Look at the map. Complete the sentences with the correct answers.**

1. The bank is ________________ Frosty's Donuts.
2. Special Electronics is next to the ________________.
3. The movie theater is on the corner of ________________ and Queen Street.
4. Mandy's Burgers is ________________ Maple Street.

D. **Work with your partner. Ask for and give directions to different places on the map.**

Where is The Coffee Cup? *Take the first right and walk . . .*

5 Role-Play

A. **Work with a partner. One person will pretend to be a police officer. The other is a tourist who has just arrived in Honolulu, Hawaii.**

Ask for directions to the following places. Use the dialog on page 18 if you need help.

How do I get to Honolulu Zoo? *Go straight on Kalakaua Avenue for five blocks, then . . .*

- Honolulu Zoo
- Kapahulu Library
- Ala Wai Canal
- Honolulu Aquarium
- Kapiolani Park
- Jefferson Elementary
- Prince Kuhio Hotel

B. **Have you ever been lost in a strange place? Work in a group. Discuss how it felt to be lost and how you solved the problem.**

I was lost in the supermarket once. I turned around and my mother was gone! I was so scared, but I went to the cashier and told her, and she put out a message on the speakers. My mom found me!

6 Partner-Up

A. Listen to the dialog and perform both roles with a partner. Track 7

Joanne: Excuse me. Is there a **grocery store** near here?

Stranger: Yes, there is **Farmer Tom's Fruits**.

Joanne: Oh, good. Do you know the way?

Stranger: Sure. Go **straight ahead and turn left** onto **North Street**.

Joanne: **North Street**, got it.

Stranger: Go straight until you see the **church**.

Joanne: OK. And the **grocery store** is there?

Stranger: The **grocery store** is **behind** the **church**.

Joanne: Thank you so much.

Stranger: That's OK. Hurry, it'll close soon!

B. With your partner, practice the dialog with the following details.

- movie theater
- King's Theater
- two blocks and turn right
- Kings Road
- high school
- across from

- train station
- East City Station
- straight and turn right
- Main Street
- bus station
- next to

- electronics store
- Ace Electronics
- right and take the first left
- Sunrise Boulevard
- Chinese restaurant
- above

C. Make up your own directions and practice the dialog again.

Integrated Learning

1 Comprehension

A. **Work with a partner. Look at the clues and the map below. Write the correct number next to each store.**

a. The movie theater is next to the bus station.
b. The karaoke club is across from the bus station.
c. The post office is next to the library.
d. The pharmacy is at the end of Prince Street.
e. The flower shop is on your right.
f. The department store is just before the karaoke club.
g. The library is on the second corner to the left.
h. The clothing store is on Prince Street.

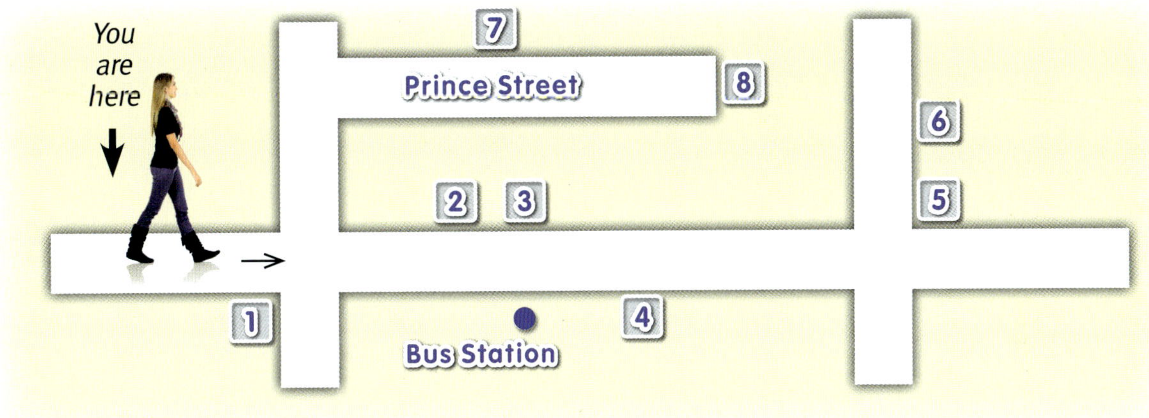

Movie Theater ☐	Karaoke Club ☐	Post Office ☐
Pharmacy ☐	Flower Shop ☐	Department Store ☐
Library ☐	Clothing Store ☐	

B. **Choose a place that you go to often. Write a letter to a friend that explains how to get there.**

You should come to the Green Fields Gym with me! Start at the train station. Turn right and walk down Railway Lane. At the intersection, turn left and go straight until you see the bookstore on your left. The gym is across from the bookstore. See you there!

C. **Work in a group. Present your writing. Ask and answer questions with your classmates.**

Practice

1 Dialog

A. Listen to the recording and write the missing words that you hear. Track 5

Sara:	Excuse me, sir. Could you help me, ______________? I'm a little lost.
Policeman:	Of course. Where do you need to go, ma'am?
Sara:	Well, I've been _____________ to find the **Sea View Shopping Arcade** for the last ___________!
Policeman:	OK. Let me help you. Go ______________ up this road until you reach the intersection.
Sara:	Pardon me? I couldn't hear you.
Policeman:	____________ up the road to the intersection. Then go straight until you see the **bank**.
Sara:	Up the intersection, walk until I see the **bank**, right.
Policeman:	Yep. The **arcade** is **across from** the ___________. You can't miss it.
Sara:	Thank you very much. You've been very helpful. I'm ________ I'll find it now.
Policeman:	My pleasure. ___________ your **shopping**, ma'am.

B. Look at the bolded words in the dialog above. With a partner, think of some new information to replace these words.

C. Practice the dialog using the new information.

2 Picture Description

Listen and choose the statement that best describes what you see in the picture. Track 8

1.

Ⓐ Ⓑ Ⓒ Ⓓ

2.

Ⓐ Ⓑ Ⓒ Ⓓ

3 Unscramble

Unscramble the sentences below.

1. next to / It's / television. / the
→ ____________________

2. get to / bank? / can I / How / the
→ ____________________

3. store / The hotel / between the / is / the gym. / and
→ ____________________

4. right, / your first / and it's / Take / the left. / on
→ ____________________

5. under / They put / Christmas tree. / the / the presents
→ ____________________

Note Taking

Main Points	Detail

Summary

Brainstorming

Journal/Activity Writing

UNIT 03 Sickness & Health

Talking About:
Being healthy and getting sick

Warm-Up

Do you think that you are healthy?
Do you exercise often?

1 Model Dialog

Listen and practice the dialog with a partner. Track 9

Ellie:	Trevor, how are you doing? I haven't seen you for a while.
Trevor:	Hey, Ellie. Yeah, I've been really sick for the last few days.
Ellie:	Oh, no, are you OK? I heard there was a virus going around. My mom was sick.
Trevor:	I guess I had that. I had a headache, a runny nose, and a bad stomach.
Ellie:	Oh, that's horrible. Are you feeling better now?
Trevor:	A little bit. I have an exam today, so I had to come in.
Ellie:	If you feel really sick, just tell your teacher. I'm sure she'll understand.
Trevor:	She won't. My teacher is Miss Anderton. She hates sick people.
Ellie:	I know her. She's super-fit, isn't she? She exercises every day.
Trevor:	And she's never sick. She'll say it's my fault! It's so unfair!

Speaking Success!

There are a few ways that we can talk about **non-specific periods of time.**

A few days
= *three or more days*

A couple (of) days = *two days*

A moment
= *a brief amount of time*

A while
= *a longer period of time*

2 Vocabulary

Work with a partner. Write the number of each body part next to its name.

face ___
forehead ___
eyebrow ___
eyelashes ___
eye ___
nose ___
ear ___
cheek ___
mouth ___
lip ___
tooth ___
chin ___
neck ___
arm ___
shoulder ___
armpit ___

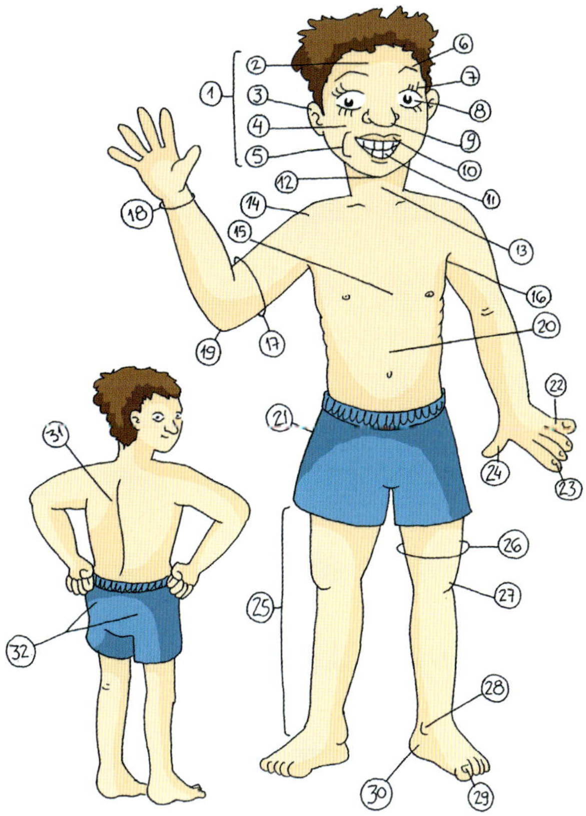

___ chest
___ elbow
___ wrist
___ finger
___ fingernail
___ thumb
___ stomach
___ hips
___ back
___ bottom
___ leg
___ thigh
___ knee
___ ankle
___ heel
___ toe

3 Essential Expressions

Look at the sentences below. Fill in the blanks with the following words.

stomachache	fever	nose
allergy	sore	toothache

1. I went to the dentist this week because I had a bad ________________.
2. I don't like summer since I have a bad pollen ________________.
3. My mom made me a honey and lemon drink for my ________________ throat.
4. The ________________ kept him in bed for a whole week.
5. She had a bad cold that week, and could hardly breathe out of her ________________.
6. He thinks that he might have gotten the ________________ from some bad sushi he ate.

4 Listening

A. Listen to Dean talking about his habits. Write a number next to each question in the order it is asked. Track 10

a. Do you have your teeth cleaned once a year? ____
b. Do you exercise at least three times a week? ____
c. Do you catch a cold more than twice a year? ____
d. Do you usually get enough sleep? ____
e. Do you eat fruits and vegetables almost every day? ____
f. Do you smoke more than three cigarettes a day? ____
g. Is work or school stressful for you? ____
h. Do you get drunk once or more per month? ____
i. Do you need to lose weight? ____
j. Do you eat junk food almost every day? ____

B. Listen again to the questions in the correct order. Does Dean answer "Yes" or "No" to these questions? Circle "Yes" or "No" below.

1. Yes No
2. Yes No
3. Yes No
4. Yes No
5. Yes No
6. Yes No
7. Yes No
8. Yes No
9. Yes No
10. Yes No

Scoring

Question	Points Yes	Points No	Question	Points Yes	Points No
1	−3	+3	6	−1	+1
2	+3	−3	7	+1	−1
3	−2	+2	8	+3	−3
4	+2	−2	9	−2	+2
5	−2	+2	10	−3	+3

Points	
10 to 20	Excellent health
0 to 9	Healthy
-1 to -9	Unhealthy
-10 to -20	Very unhealthy

C. Look at the points system above, and Dean's answers from Activity B. Work out how many points he gets. How healthy is Dean?

D. Work with a partner. Ask and answer questions that Dean is asked. Look at your score. How healthy are you?

I don't smoke at all, and I don't drink alcohol. I . . .

5 Survey

A. **Work with a partner. Talk about and match each symptom to the related illness.**

1. My throat hurts when I swallow. •	• a. a stomachache
2. My eyes itch and I sneeze a lot. •	• b. a headache
3. My ear hurts. •	• c. a backache
4. My stomach hurts. •	• d. an allergy
5. My head aches. •	• e. an earache
6. My back hurts. •	• f. a fever
7. I feel very hot. •	• g. a sore throat
8. My tooth hurts. •	• h. a toothache

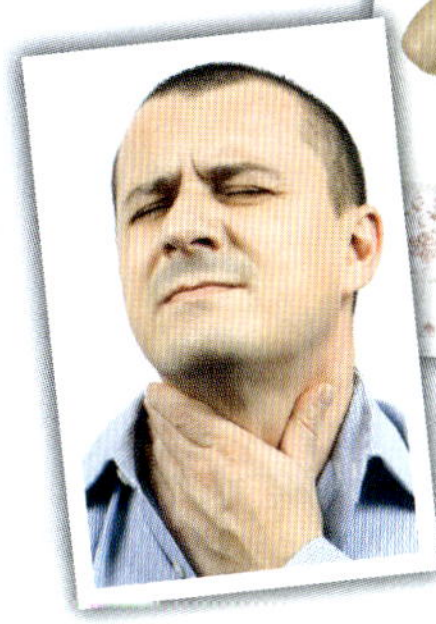

B. **Find two classmates. Ask the following questions. Write their responses.**

	NAME ________	NAME ________
How good is your eyesight?		
When was the last time you threw up?		
How often do you get a headache?		
Do you have any allergies?		
Do you ever get motion sickness?		
What's the highest temperature you've ever had?		
What's something that makes you feel dizzy?		
What's something that makes you feel nauseous?		
Have you ever been in the hospital? What for?		
Have you ever broken a bone? How did it happen?		

C. **Work in a group. Discuss your answers to the questions.**

6 Partner-Up

A. Work with a partner. Look at the crossword below. One of you is partner A, and the other is Partner B. Cover up your partner's clues. Give each other clues and attempt to complete the crossword.

Partner A

Down hints

1. Feeling as if you might throw up.
3. The upper part of your leg.
6. When you are sick, this will be high.
7. A hole in your tooth.
8. A reflex action that causes quick short breaths.

Partner B

Across hints

2. You are sneezing, and you have itchy, watery eyes.
4. The world feels like it is spinning.
5. It hurts when you swallow.
8. You have a pain in your head.
9. Your body aches and you have a fever, you are very tired.
10. To push air from the lungs suddenly and with a loud noise.
11. If these hurt, you may have trouble hearing.

B. Work in a group. Compare your answers.

C. Your teacher will give you the correct answers. How many did you get correct?

Integrated Learning

1 Comprehension

A. Listen to Hayley talk about the health problems that she has experienced. Write down her answers to these questions. Track 11

1. How often does she get a cold? ______________________
2. How often does she get a headache? ______________________
3. When was the last time she had the flu? ______________________
4. Does she have any allergies? ______________________
5. Why was she in the hospital? ______________________
6. What's something that makes her feel nauseous? ______________________
7. What's something that makes her feel dizzy? ______________________

B. Work in a group. Discuss Hayley's health, and compare it to your own.

I think Hayley is reasonably healthy. She seems to have had many illnesses, but . . .

C. Let's play a game! Play in a group.

- Silently act out an illness or health condition. No speaking!
- Your teammates will try to guess the illness.
- Whoever guesses correctly acts out next.
- Use other illness words from this unit when you have finished those on this page.

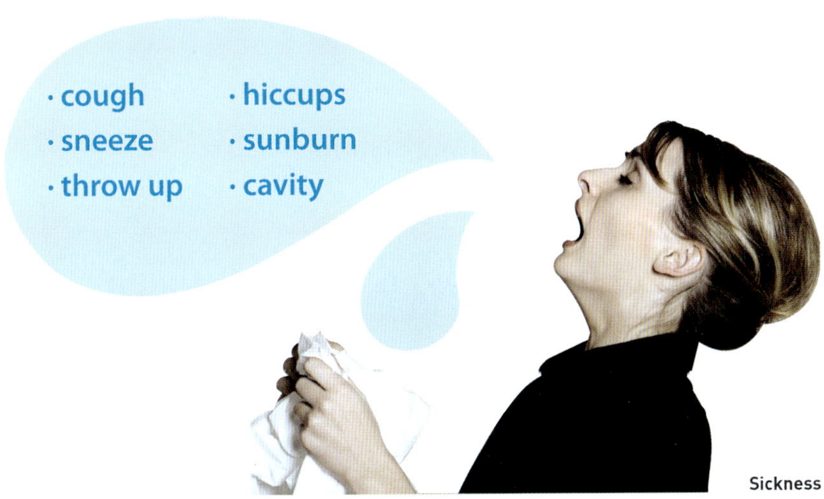

Practice

1 Dialog

A. Listen to the recording and write the missing words that you hear. Track 9

Ellie:	Trevor, how are you ____________? I haven't seen you for a ________.
Trevor:	Hey, Ellie. Yeah, I've been ________ sick for the last few days.
Ellie:	Oh, no, are you OK? I heard there was a virus going around. My mom was sick.
Trevor:	I ________ I had that. I had a **headache**, runny nose, and a **bad stomach**.
Ellie:	Oh, that's horrible. Are you feeling __________ now?
Trevor:	A little bit. I have an exam **today**, so I had to come in.
Ellie:	If you feel really sick, just tell your teacher. I'm sure she'll ____________.
Trevor:	She won't. My teacher is **Miss Anderton**. She hates sick people.
Ellie:	I know her. She's super-fit, isn't she? She ____________ every day.
Trevor:	And she's ___________ sick. She'll say it's my fault! It's so **unfair**!

B. Look at the bolded words in the dialog above. With a partner, think of some new information to replace these words.

C. Practice the dialog using the new information.

2 Picture Description

Listen and choose the statement that best describes what you see in the picture. Track 12

1.

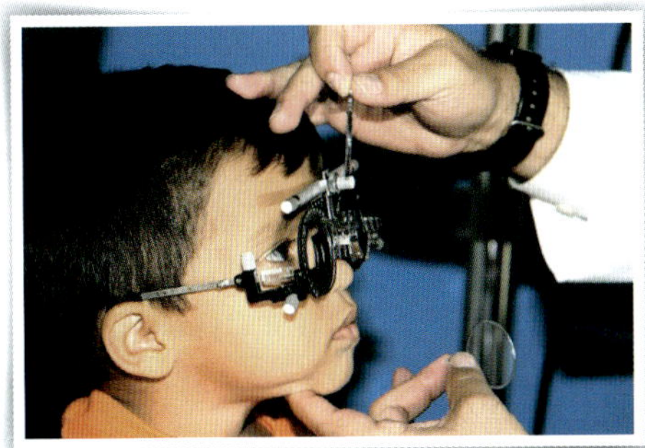

Ⓐ Ⓑ Ⓒ Ⓓ

2.

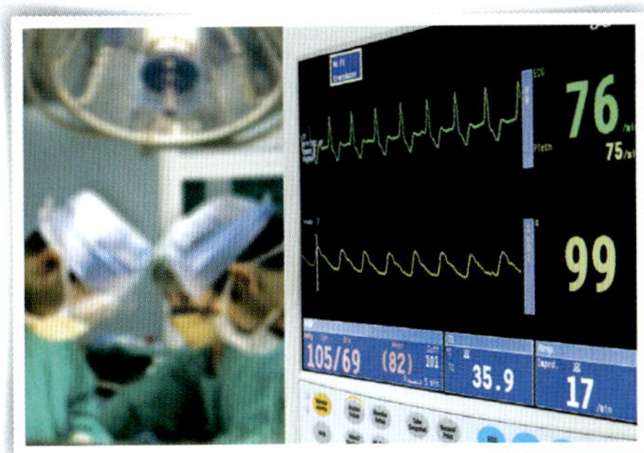

Ⓐ Ⓑ Ⓒ Ⓓ

3 Unscramble

Unscramble the sentences below.

1. was young, / When I / got / really bad / I / headaches.
   → ______________________________

2. allergies? / have / you / any / Do
   → ______________________________

3. ever / Have you / hospital? / go to / had to / the
   → ______________________________

4. hours of / How many / sleep / usually get? / do you
   → ______________________________

5. bad / I / back. / a / have
   → ______________________________

Note Taking

Main Points	Detail

Summary

Brainstorming

Journal/Activity Writing

UNIT 04 Cooking

Warm-Up

Who usually cooks in your house?
What is one food you can cook?

Talking About:
Describing foods and how to cook them

1 Model Dialog

Listen and practice the dialog with a partner. Track 13

Louis: Good morning. Mmm . . . something smells good!
Leslie: Yeah, I'm frying some bacon and making scrambled eggs.
Louis: Oh, yummy! I love bacon, but I don't know how to make scrambled eggs.
Leslie: You don't know? I'll teach you! Crack a few eggs into a bowl, and add some milk.
Louis: Got it. Then whisk the eggs together, right?
Leslie: That's right. Beat them until the yolk and the white are mixed together.
Louis: And then I guess I need some seasoning, don't I?
Leslie: Yes! Add in some salt and pepper. I think you know how to do this.
Louis: Well, I've watched my dad do it a few times. I guess I picked it up.
Leslie: Then add some butter to a heated pan and pour in the mixture. Delicious!

Speaking Success!

If we want clarification on something, we can turn a **statement into a question** by adding the following words.

Then whisk the eggs together, **right?**

I need some seasoning, **don't I?**

He should, **shouldn't he?**

2 Vocabulary

A. **Match the cooking verbs to the correct picture.**

boil fry chop grate stir peel beat bake simmer

1. ______________

2. ______________

3. ______________

4. ______________

5. ______________

6. ______________

7. ______________

8. ______________

9. ______________

B. **Work with a partner. For each verb, think of two foods that can be cooked in that way.**

*You can **boil** potatoes and eggs. You can **bake** pies and cakes . . .*

3 Essential Expressions

Look at the sentences below. Fill in the blanks with the following words.

fry	peel	chop	bake	grate

1. First, use a knife to ______________ the carrots into small pieces.
2. Add the olive oil and onions to the hot pan ______________ them.
3. Put the cake in the oven and ______________ for one hour.
4. Boil the tomatoes for one minute so it is easier to ______________ off the skin.
5. As a finishing touch, ______________ some cheese over the top of the dish.

4 Listening

A. Look at the picture. What do these people do? Would you like to do their job?

B. Listen to some foods being described. Try to guess the foods. Write them below. Track 14

1.	2.	3.
4.	5.	6.
7.	8.	9.
10.	11.	12.

C. Compare your answers with a partner. Then listen and check your answers. Track 15

D. Choose one of the foods below. Describe it to your partner. Your partner will try to guess which food you are talking about. Think of your own foods as well.

These are kind of round, and they can be red or green. They are crunchy and sweet, too— *Apples!*

- apple
- rice
- bread
- grape
- cereal
- bacon
- pizza
- orange juice
- chocolate
- banana
- egg

5 Interview

A. Choose a partner. Ask him/her the following questions and write the responses in full sentences.

1. Can you cook?

   ____

2. What foods can you cook?

   ____

3. Do you think you are a good cook?

   ____

4. Do you like cooking?

   ____

5. What don't you like about cooking?

   ____

6. Who is the best cook that you know?

   ____

7. What is your favorite meal? Describe why you like it.

   ____

8. Do you prefer eating out or cooking at home?

   ____

9. Do you like spicy foods?

   ____

10. Do you prefer sweet or savory foods?

    ____

B. Work in a group. Discuss your partner's responses.

William says he does not like cooking, but I love it! I can cook . . .

6 Partner-Up

A. **This is a recipe for potato salad. Work with a partner. Look at the pictures. Number the instructions in the correct order.**

Susan's "World's Best" Potato Salad

Ingredients

- *4–5 potatoes*
- *1/4 cup carrot*
- *1/3 cup black olives*
- *1 tbsp. onion*
- *3 tbsp. celery*
- *3 tbsp. sweet relish*
- *1 tbsp. French mustard*
- *2 tsp. vinegar*
- *1 tbsp. Italian dressing*
- *1 cup mayonnaise*
- *2 eggs*
- *salt + pepper*

Recipe

- ☐ Cover and chill for three hours.
- ☐ Add onion, celery, carrot, and sweet relish.
- ☐ Boil eggs for fifteen minutes, peel and chop.
- ☐ Pour vinegar over potatoes.
- ☐ Mix mayonnaise, Italian dressing, and mustard.
- ☐ Boil potatoes in salted water until soft.
- ☐ Peel onions and chop finely.
- ☐ Carefully stir in eggs and olives.
- ☐ Add salt and pepper to taste.
- ☐ Chop celery, slice olives, and shred carrot.
- ☐ Add mayonnaise mixture to potatoes and stir lightly.
- ☐ Peel and cube boiled potatoes and put in a large bowl.

B. **Now, cover the steps and tell your partner the recipe. Look only at the pictures.**

Integrated Learning

1 Comprehension

A. Look at Susan's potato salad recipe. Think of a dish that you can cook, or make one up. Write the recipe below.

First, choose a name for your dish: ______________________

Then list your ingredients:

______________________ ______________________

______________________ ______________________

______________________ ______________________

______________________ ______________________

______________________ ______________________

Finally, write down your recipe. Use the cooking verbs from page 39:

____

____

____

____

____

____

____

____

____

____

B. In small groups, describe how to make your recipe. Use the sequence markers from page 12 to help you.

First, chop up the onions and carrots. Next, heat the frying pan and pour in some oil . . .

C. Present your recipe to the class.

Practice

1 Dialog

A. Listen to the recording and write the missing words that you hear. Track 13

Louis: Good morning. Mmm . . . something ________ good!

Leslie: Yeah, I'm ________ some **bacon** and ________ **scrambled eggs**.

Louis: Oh, yummy! I love bacon, but I don't ________ how to make **scrambled eggs**.

Leslie: You don't know? I'll __________ you! **Crack a few eggs into a bowl**, and **add some milk**.

Louis: Got it. Then **whisk the eggs together**, right?

Leslie: That's right. **Beat them until the yolk and the white are** ________ together.

Louis: And then I guess I need some seasoning, don't I?

Leslie: Yes! Add in some salt and pepper. I think you know how to do this.

Louis: Well, I've ______________ my dad do it a few times. I guess I picked it up.

Leslie: Then add some butter to a heated pan and **pour in the mixture**. ________!

B. Look at the bolded words in the dialog above. With a partner, think of some new information to replace these words.

C. Practice the dialog using the new information.

2 Picture Description

Listen and choose the statement that best describes what you see in the picture. Track 16

1. 

Ⓐ Ⓑ Ⓒ Ⓓ

2. 

Ⓐ Ⓑ Ⓒ Ⓓ

3 Unscramble

Unscramble the sentences below.

1. I / the curry / was too / couldn't eat / because it / spicy!

→ ______________________________

2. breakfast. / orange juice / usually have / cereal and / for / I

→ ______________________________

3. tasty, but / Pizza / it is not / is / healthy.

→ ______________________________

4. favorite / meal is / spaghetti / My / bolognese.

→ ______________________________

5. allergic / Mary / to / is / shellfish.

→ ______________________________

Note Taking

Main Points	Detail

Summary

Brainstorming

Journal/Activity Writing

UNIT 05 Around the World

Warm-Up

Name each of the earth's continents.
How many countries can you name on each continent?

Talking About:
Different cultures and countries

1 Model Dialog

Listen and practice the dialog with a partner. Track 17

Gemma:	Muhammad, how are you doing? You look excited.
Muhammad:	Oh, I am! Very! Today is Eid. It's my favorite day of the year.
Gemma:	Eid? What's that? Is it like Christmas?
Muhammad:	Well, it's a Muslim holiday, to celebrate the end of Ramadan.
Gemma:	Oh, yes. Ramadan is when you fast during the day, isn't it?
Muhammad:	Yes, it's like Lent for Christians. So, Eid is like Easter, I guess.
Gemma:	Do you eat a lot of delicious food? And play music?
Muhammad:	Yes, we have a huge feast, and we party and celebrate all day.
Gemma:	That sounds like a lot of fun! I wish I could go!
Muhammad:	Oh, why don't you join me? My mother always makes too much food.
Gemma:	No, I couldn't. I didn't fast, so it's not for me! Have fun, though!
Muhammad:	Thanks! See you later, Gemma.

Speaking Success!

When writing, **exclamation points** are used to signify strong emotions or shouting.

Oh, I am!

Very!

Have fun, though!

Thanks!

2 Vocabulary

A. Look at the list of different nations. Turn the nations into nationalities. Work with a partner if you get stuck.

Tip: These word endings are most common in nationalities:
-ese, -ish, -ian, -an, -er

1. Japan ________	2. Germany ________	3. China ________
4. Australia ________	5. Taiwan ________	6. Russia ________
7. USA ________	8. Spain ________	9. New Zealand ________
10. Brazil ________	11. Mexico ________	12. England ________

B. Listen and check your answers. Track 18

C. Work with your partner. Talk about these countries. What do you know about their cultures?

I know that many stores in ***France*** *and* ***Spain*** *close for up to two hours to have lunch. It sounds great!*

3 Essential Expressions

Look at the sentences below. Fill in the blanks with the following words.

China	Brazil	Germany's	Australia
Spain	New Zealand	USA	Japan

1. ________ has over one billion citizens.
2. The first president of the ________ was George Washington.
3. ________ is famous for its carnival.
4. Judo and karate both come from ________.
5. The famous soccer team FC Barcelona comes from ________.
6. ________ is famous for animals like the kangaroo.
7. The popular *Lord of the Rings* movies were filmed in ________.
8. Sausage and beer are examples of ________ cuisine.

4 Listening

A. **Look at these cultural foods below. Which countries do they come from? Write the country underneath the picture. Check with a partner.**

Tacos

Enchiladas

1. ______________________

Peking Duck

Wonton Soup

2. ______________________

Tandoori Chicken

Chicken Curry

3. ______________________

Ravioli

Pizza

4. ______________________

Galbi

Bibimbap

5. ______________________

Green Curry

Tom Yam Kung

6. ______________________

B. **Listen to Rebecca answer questions about the cultural foods above. Write her responses.**

Track 19

1. Which country's food is Rebecca's favorite? ______________________
2. Which Mexican foods can Rebecca make? ______________________
3. How does Rebecca make nachos? ______________________
4. In which country did she live for a year? ______________________
5. What is in wonton soup? ______________________
6. Which Italian foods can Rebecca make? ______________________
7. Which two countries' food has she not tried? ______________________

C. **Work in a group. Talk about Rebecca's responses. Give your own opinions.**

Rebecca has never eaten Indian food, but it's my favorite! I love curry and naan and . . .

D. **Which country's food is your favorite? Discuss in your group.**

American food is not healthy, but it's so tasty. Spain has a lot of delicious . . .

5 Quiz

A. **Work with a partner. First, add two more trivia questions to your list. Then take turns asking and answering the questions.**

Partner A

1. Berlin is the capital city of which country?
2. Which country is shaped like a boot?
3. What are the two most common languages in Singapore?
4. What is the largest continent on Earth?
5. Which language has the largest number of native speakers?
6. In which country is the island of Bali?
7. What language do people speak in Brazil?
8. ______________________________
9. ______________________________

Partner B

1. Bangkok is the capital city of which country?
2. Which country is famous for having more sheep than people?
3. Which country was Gandhi from?
4. What's the largest city in Mexico?
5. What is the largest island in the world?
6. Which country hosted the 1988 Olympics?
7. What are three major countries that use dollars?
8. ______________________________
9. ______________________________

B. **Listen to the answers. Discuss them with your class. Who got most answers correct?**

Track 20

6 Partner-Up

A. The people below are speaking in their native languages. Where are they from? What languages are they speaking? Work with a partner.

Ernesto

Riza

Ahmed

Gai

Ravi

Gyeong-mi

Peter

Mandisa

Where's Ernesto from? *He's from Mexico.*
What language does he speak? *He speaks Spanish.*

B. Let's play a game! Play with your partner.

- Look at the country cards from page 125.
- Shuffle them and put them face down.
- Choose a country and show your partner. Ask your partner to give you as many facts about that country as he/she can.
- The player with the most points is the winner!

CANADA

Canada is in North America.
Canadians speak English and French.
Canada is near the US.
Montreal is a big city there.
Hockey is a popular sport there.

Integrated Learning

1 Comprehension

A. **Work with a partner. Read the passage below. Take turns reading it aloud.**

Saint Patrick is the patron saint of Ireland. He used the shamrock, a three-leaved plant, as a symbol. On March 17th, Irish people in Ireland, and all over the world, celebrate St. Patrick's Day. People wear shamrocks and dress all in green. It is popular worldwide. People drink Guinness, which is a thick, creamy, and bitter-tasting beer with a black color. I don't like it, but I still love Saint Patrick's Day! It's a great day to get together with friends and family. And it's a public holiday in Ireland, so we don't have to go to class!

B. **Read again. Answer the questions. Use full sentences.**

1. Who is the patron saint of Ireland? ______________________________
2. When is Saint Patrick's Day? ______________________________
3. What color do people wear on St. Patrick's Day? ______________________________
4. What did St. Patrick use as a symbol? ______________________________
5. Is St. Patrick's Day a public holiday in Ireland? ______________________________
6. What is Guinness like? ______________________________

C. **Write about a cultural event that is specific to your own country. You can write about another country's festivities if you know of any.**

D. **Work in a group. Present and discuss your writing.**

Practice

1 Dialog

A. Listen to the recording and write the missing words that you hear. Track 17

Gemma:	Muhammad, how are you doing? You look ______________.
Muhammad:	Oh, I am! Very! Today is **Eid**. It's my _____________ day of the year.
Gemma:	Eid? What's that? Is it like **Christmas**?
Muhammad:	Well, it's a **Muslim** ___________ to celebrate **the end of Ramadan**.
Gemma:	Oh, yes. **Ramadan** is ________ **you fast during the day**, isn't it?
Muhammad:	Yes, it's like **Lent for Christians**. So **Eid is like Easter**, I guess.
Gemma:	Do you eat a lot of delicious food? And play music?
Muhammad:	Yes, we have a huge feast, and we **party** and ____________ all day.
Gemma:	That ___________ like a lot of fun! I wish I could go!
Muhammad:	Oh, why don't you join me? My mother always makes ________ much food.
Gemma:	No, I couldn't. I didn't fast, so it's not for me! Have fun, ________!
Muhammad:	Thanks! See you later, Gemma.

B. Look at the bolded words in the dialog above. With a partner, think of some new information to replace these words.

C. Practice the dialog using the new information.

2 Picture Description

Listen and choose the statement that best describes what you see in the picture. Track 21

1\. 

Ⓐ Ⓑ Ⓒ Ⓓ

2\. 

Ⓐ Ⓑ Ⓒ Ⓓ

3 Unscramble

Unscramble the sentences below.

1. vegetables. / Bibimbap / Korean food / made with / is a / rice and
   → ______________________________

2. is Brasilia. / city of / capital / Brazil / The
   → ______________________________

3. love / Indian food, / I / prawn curry. / especially
   → ______________________________

4. year / went to / the Philippines / Last / I / vacation. / on
   → ______________________________

5. go to / Canada / I would / someday. / love / to
   → ______________________________

Note Taking

Main Points	Detail

Summary

Brainstorming

Journal/Activity Writing

UNIT 06 Telling Stories

Warm-Up

Talk about something memorable that happened to you recently.

Talking About:

Things that have happened to us

1 Model Dialog

Listen and practice the dialog with a partner. Track 22

Josh: Did you have a good weekend, Cheryl? You went to the beach, right?

Cheryl: Well, I was going to go with my sisters. But the weather was awful.

Josh: Yeah, it was. Did you do something else instead?

Cheryl: Yes, we had traveled all the way to the beach, so we went to the Sea View Arcade.

Josh: That's a shopping center, isn't it?

Cheryl: Yep, it's huge. We spent ages looking at the sales, and we each got a manicure.

Josh: That sounds nice. My weekend was terrible.

Cheryl: Oh, really? How so?

Josh: I got stood up on a blind date. Then I was late to work on Sunday, and I got fired!

Cheryl: Oh, no! Did your alarm clock not go off?

Josh: Yeah, I think the batteries died. Well, I'm off to look for a new job!

Speaking Success!

There are certain common **idioms** and **phrasal verbs** that are used to talk about everyday occurrences.

To stand (someone) up
= *to miss an appointment*

To get fired
= *to be removed from one's job*

To go off = *to start ringing*

2 Vocabulary

A. Listen to the pronunciation of these regular simple past verbs. Write each verb in the correct column according to its pronunciation. Track 23

visited	promised	moved	played	performed	laughed
walked	brushed	showed	cried	graduated	liked

/d/	/t/	/id/
______	______	______
______	______	______
______	______	______
______	______	______
______	______	______

B. Work with a partner. Make sentences with these words.

*I **promised** to see my grandmother on the weekend, so I **visited** her on Sunday.*

3 Essential Expressions

Look at the sentences below. Fill in the blanks with the following words.

promised	graduated	walked	visited
showed	played	liked	spend

1. Last week I ______ my cousins in Alabama.
2. It was a dark night, so I ______ home with my friend to feel safer.
3. Her younger sister ______ from college last month.
4. They ______ each other that they would always be friends.
5. They had to ______ the weekend packing up boxes before they moved.
6. Rachel ______ this house much more than her old one.
7. He ______ them the present he had bought for his wife.
8. The three of them ______ video games all day long.

4 Listening

A. **Listen as Lewis talks about some things he did yesterday. Check "True or "False" for each item.** Track 24

	True	False
1. He got up before 9:00.		
2. He ate breakfast.		
3. He checked his email.		
4. He did laundry.		
5. He washed his car.		
6. He worked out at the gym.		
7. He played basketball.		
8. He went shopping.		
9. He went to a movie.		
10. He went to bed before midnight.		

B. **Turn the above statements into *Yes/No* questions. Ask a partner what Lewis did yesterday.**

Did he get up before 9:00? *Yes, he did.* (True) / *No, he didn't.* (False)

C. **Think of some more *Yes/No* questions. Ask your partner about the past.**

Did you watch television yesterday? *Yes, I did. I watched a soap opera.*

5 Story Time

A. Work in a group. Look at the two stories below. In your groups, take turns adding new sentences to the stories. Make sure to use the simple past.

It was a hot, humid night. A man walked into a restaurant. When he sat down, he saw a beautiful woman sitting across the room . . .

Ruby just finished working twelve hours. She walked to the station and got on a jam-packed train . . .

B. Look at the pictures below. Work with a partner. Choose at least two of the following pictures. Make up a story using these images and the words provided.

take
bath
ring

1

2

play
see
miss

play
lightning
start

3

4

swim
see
shark

ride
stranger
ask

5

6
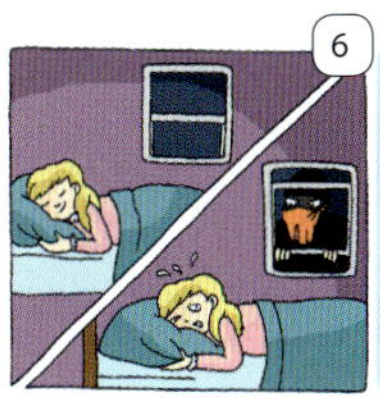

sleep
burglar
come

C. With your partner, tell your story to the group.

6 Partner-Up

A. **Mr. Parker is very angry. Yesterday his students behaved very badly during class! Write the simple past forms of these verbs.**

1. talk ____________
2. sleep ____________
3. read ____________
4. listen ____________
5. play ____________
6. chew ____________
7. put on ____________
8. copy ____________
9. blow ____________

B. **Work with a partner. Look at the image and talk about what each person did wrong. Use the simple past.**

What did this girl do wrong? *She talked on the phone.*

C. **Now do the same, using the past progressive tense. Look at page 11 if you need a reminder.**

What was he doing? *He was sleeping on his desk.*

D. **Did you ever do anything bad at school? Discuss in a group.**

I was mostly a very good student in middle school, but one day I . . .

Integrated Learning

1 Comprehension

A. Read the story below. Fill in the blanks with the simple past form of these verbs.

have   see   be   go

One night, a bald man 1______ at a party. He 2______ a handsome young man. The man 3______ lots of hair and 4______ very popular with women.

The bald man 5______ sad because when he 6______ young he 7______ lots of hair and 8______ lots of girlfriends, too.

The next morning, he 9______ to a toupee shop to buy a toupee.

B. Complete the story, using your own imagination. Draw pictures and describe what is happening in each panel. Make sure to use the simple past.

____
____
____
____

____
____
____
____

____
____
____
____

C. Work in a group. Present your story.

Practice

1 Dialog

A. Listen to the recording and write the missing words that you hear. Track 22

Jacob: Did you have a good ___________, Cheryl? You went to **the beach**, right?

Cheryl: Well, I was going to go with my ________. But the weather was __________.

Jacob: Yeah, it was. Did you do something else instead?

Cheryl: Yes, we had _____________ all the way to **the beach**, so we went to the **Sea View Arcade**.

Jacob: That's a **shopping center**, isn't it?

Cheryl: Yep, it's huge. We spent _______ looking at the **sales**, and we each got a **manicure**.

Jacob: That sounds nice. My weekend was _______________.

Cheryl: Oh, really? How so?

Jacob: I got **stood up on a blind date**. Then I was late to work on _____________, and I got fired!

Cheryl: Oh, no! Did your alarm clock not go off?

Jacob: Yeah, I think the batteries _______. Well, I'm off to look for a new job!

B. Look at the bolded words in the dialog above. With a partner, think of some new information to replace these words.

C. Practice the dialog using the new information.

2 Picture Description

Listen and choose the statement that best describes what you see in the picture. Track 25

1.

Ⓐ Ⓑ Ⓒ Ⓓ

2.

Ⓐ Ⓑ Ⓒ Ⓓ

3 Unscramble

Unscramble the sentences below.

1. I bought / for my / Yesterday / a new / mother. / sewing machine
   → ______________________________

2. how to / My sister / fix a / taught me / broken fusebox.
   → ______________________________

3. feel sick / too much / I / last night. / as I / this morning, / drank
   → ______________________________

4. sang beautifully / Melissa / school performance / last night. / in the
   → ______________________________

5. think about / and he / I spoke / said he / would / to the / it. / principal,
   → ______________________________

Note Taking

Main Points	Detail

Summary

Brainstorming

Journal/Activity Writing

UNIT 07 Eating Out

Warm-Up

What was the last restaurant you went to?
What did you order?

Talking About:
Eating at a restaurant

1 Model Dialog

Listen and practice the dialog with a partner. Track 26

Melody: Are you hungry, Billy? I'm absolutely starving!
Billy: Yeah, me, too. But I don't think we have anything in the fridge.
Melody: How about if we go out? There's a new Chinese place round the corner.
Billy: Chinese? Hmm. . . how about Indian food?
Melody: Indian food? Oh no, I can't eat that. It's much too spicy for me!
Billy: They have lots of other stuff, too. The waiters there are very helpful.
Melody: How about something else? Pizza, maybe?
Billy: We had pizza yesterday! I want Indian food.
Melody: Well, I want Chinese! Let's both go and buy takeout, and eat it back here.
Billy: Sure! I prefer eating at home to eating out, actually.
Melody: Yeah, this way we can eat at home, but there are no dishes to wash. Let's go!
Billy: Great!

Speaking Success!

Hyperbole is the use of exaggeration for emphasis. What is said is not meant to be taken literally.

I'm starving! = *I'm very hungry.*

This bag weighs a ton!
= *This bag is very heavy.*

I've told you a thousand times
= *I've told you many times.*

2 Vocabulary

Look at the menu for Buster's restaurant below. Fill in the menu with the correct words.

beverages sandwiches chicken chocolate roast desserts main meals cooked

BUSTER'S

1) ________________

Served with your choice of *salad, rice, or baked potato.*

TERIYAKI STEAK
Tender and juicy. Marinated in our Oriental teriyaki sauce.
14.95

MUSHROOM 2) ____________
Chicken baked in a delicious, creamy mushroom sauce.
10.95

3) __________ **BEEF**
Delicious and juicy.
13.95

HAMBURGER STEAK
8 ounces of ground beef 4) ________ to perfection
9.95

5) ________________

Served with your choice of *French fries or onion rings*

CHICKEN SANDWICH 6.50
GRILLED CHEESE SANDWICH 3.95
TUNA SANDWICH 4.95
HAMBURGER 5.75
w/cheese 6.50

6) ________________

YUMMY PIES 2.95
HOT FUDGE SUNDAE 3.95
SHAKE 2.45
CHEESECAKE 3.50
8) ____________ CAKE 3.75

7) ________________

COFFEE *or* TEA 2.25
COLA, LEMONADE 1.65
BEER 2.75
WINE 3.00
MIXED DRINKS 3.75

3 Essential Expressions

Look at the sentences below. Fill in the blanks with the following words.

slice	dessert	turkey	beverage
fried	salmon	well-done	ate out

1. You can have your steak cooked rare, medium, or ________________.
2. I want fish, so I will have the ________________ as my main meal, please.
3. Would you like ice cream for ________________?
4. Gary eats ________________ chicken a few times every month.
5. For Christmas this year I will cook a roast goose instead of a ________________.
6. I would just like a small ________________ of chocolate cake, please.
7. Would you like a ________________ to go with your meal, sir?
8. I didn't have time to make a sandwich this morning, so I ________________ for lunch.

4 Listening

A. Listen to Anna talking about the places she likes to eat. Complete the questions that she is asked. Track 27

1. What kind of ____________do you ____________ go to?
2. What's a restaurant you like that isn't very ____________?
3. What ________ ________ ________ do they have?
4. What ____________ do you usually order when you go out for ____________?
5. When you ____________ a salad, what kind of ____________ do you usually get?
6. What's a ____________ you ____________ order?
7. Do you usually pay ____________ or use a ____________ ____________ when you eat out?
8. Do you ____________ leave a __________ tip?

B. Listen again. Write down Anna's responses to the above questions.

1. ______________________________
2. ______________________________
3. ______________________________
4. ______________________________
5. ______________________________
6. ______________________________
7. ______________________________
8. ______________________________

C. Ask and answer these questions with a partner.

What's a dessert you often order? *I often order cheesecake, or . . .*

D. Anna always leaves a large tip. Do people tip in your country? What do you think about tipping? Discuss in a group.

People in my country don't leave tips. I see why people do it, but I think . . .

5 Interview

A. **Talk to a classmate. Ask him/her the following questions about eating out, and write the responses.**

1. What is the strangest food you have ever eaten?

____

2. What is the nicest restaurant you have been to?

____

3. What kind of restaurant do you usually go to?

____

4. What is the most unpleasant experience you have had at a restaurant?

____

5. What is the most expensive restaurant you have ever been to?

____

6. Do you prefer going to a restaurant or ordering takeout?

____

7. What are three ways that eating out is better than cooking at home?

a. ______________________________

b. ______________________________

c. ______________________________

8. What are three ways that cooking at home is better than eating out?

a. ______________________________

b. ______________________________

c. ______________________________

B. **Work in a group. Talk about what you found out about your classmates.**

The strangest food that Joe has ever eaten was . . .

C. **Debate: Divide your class into two groups. One group will argue that eating out is better, and the other will argue for cooking at home. Your teacher will judge which group made the better argument.**

We think eating at home is better, because it is cheaper and . . .

6 Partner-Up

A. The person below is making a reservation at a restaurant. Use the words below to fill in the dialog.

Friday three non-smoking Swanson may 7:00

Host: Good evening, this is Keo's. ________ I help you?

Customer: Yes, I'd like to reserve a table for this ________ at _______.

Host: Certainly. For how many?

Customer: For __________ people.

Host: OK. Would you like smoking or non-smoking?

Customer: _________________, please.

Host: And could I have your name, please?

Customer: My name's Bill ___________.

Host: Thank you, Mr. _____________. I've reserved a table for ______________ on___________ at _____________.

Customer: Thank you. Goodbye.

Host: Goodbye, see you on __________!

B. Listen to the recording and check your answers. Repeat the dialog with a partner. Track 28

C. Look at these other restaurants, and make a reservation with your partner. Use the dialog above as a guide.

THAI ELEPHANT

One of the best Thai restaurants in the world. Many famous movie stars have eaten here!

Phone: 951-9355

COMPADRES

Voted "Best Mexican Restaurant" four years running. Delicious Mexican food that you'll never forget.

Phone: 591-8307

HEE HING

One of the most popular Chinese restaurants in town. A huge variety of Chinese dishes.

Phone: 735-5544

CHEZ MICHEL

One of our city's most enjoyable French restaurants. French dining at its finest.

Phone: 955-7866

Integrated Learning

1 Comprehension

A. **Work in a group of four. One person is a waiter/waitress. This person must take an order from each customer and total each check. Each customer must order a main meal, a beverage, and a dessert, and leave a tip.**

Use these expressions as a guide:

- Do you accept debit cards?
- What would you recommend?
- That will be . . .
- Will that be all?
- What is today's special?
- May I take your order?

Customer 1

BUSTER'S

CHECK

DATE	TABLE NO.	NO. OF PERSONS	CHECK NO. 701

	TOTAL	

Thank you! Please come again.

Customer 2

BUSTER'S

CHECK

DATE	TABLE NO.	NO. OF PERSONS	CHECK NO. 702

	TOTAL	

Thank you! Please come again.

Customer 3

BUSTER'S

CHECK

DATE	TABLE NO.	NO. OF PERSONS	CHECK NO. 703

	TOTAL	

Thank you! Please come again.

B. **Think of your own restaurant. Create a menu for it.**

Name: ____________________

Starters	Price
____________	________
____________	________

Dessert	Price
____________	________
____________	________

Main Course	Price
____________	________
____________	________
____________	________

Beverages	Price
____________	________
____________	________

C. **Have a partner order from your menu. You will be the waiter/waitress.**

Practice

1 Dialog

A. Listen to the recording and write the missing words that you hear. Track 26

Melody:	Are you ____________, Billy? I'm absolutely starving!
Billy:	Yeah, me, too. But I don't think we have ___________ in the fridge.
Melody:	How ________ if we go out? There's a new **Chinese** place round the corner.
Billy:	Chinese? Hmm . . . how about **Indian** food?
Melody:	**Indian** food? Oh no, I can't eat that. It's much too **spicy** for me!
Billy:	They have lots of other ________, too. The waiters there are very helpful.
Melody:	How about something else? **Pizza**, maybe?
Billy:	We had **pizza** _____________! I want Indian food.
Melody:	Well, I want **Chinese**! Let's both go and buy takeout, and eat it back here.
Billy:	Sure! I __________ eating at home to eating out, actually.
Melody:	Yeah, this way we can eat at___________, but there are no dishes to ___________. Let's go!
Billy:	Great!

B. Look at the bolded words in the dialog above. With a partner, think of some new information to replace these words.

C. Practice the dialog using the new information.

2 Picture Description

Listen and choose the statement that best describes what you see in the picture. Track 29

1. 

Ⓐ Ⓑ Ⓒ Ⓓ

2. 

Ⓐ Ⓑ Ⓒ Ⓓ

3 Unscramble

Unscramble the sentences below.

1. going to / with my / I am / an Indian / boyfriend. / restaurant

→ ______________________________

2. last year, / my family / birthday / to a / For my / took me / sushi restaurant.

→ ______________________________

3. usually cook / on weekdays. / I / myself / for

→ ______________________________

4. likes to / when she / order a / goes out. / dessert / Louise

→ ______________________________

5. specials? / today's / are / What

→ ______________________________

Note Taking

Main Points	Detail

Summary

Brainstorming

Journal/Activity Writing

UNIT 08 Unreal Situations

Talking About:
Imagined events

Warm-Up

Imagine you just won 50 million dollars in the lottery!
What would you do?

1 Model Dialog

Listen and practice the dialog with a partner. Track 30

Scott: Fran, can I ask you something? If you're not busy.
Fran: Sure, go ahead. I'm not doing anything right now.
Scott: Well, what would happen if I told you your breath smelled really bad?
Fran: What would happen? Wait, does my breath smell, Scott? Is that what you're saying?
Scott: No, no! Actually, I know someone who really likes me, but her breath stinks.
Fran: Hmm . . . why don't you just tell her that her breath smells?
Scott: I can't tell her that! If I did, she'd be upset! Really upset.
Fran: Yeah. Not cool. You can't say that about someone, can you?
Scott: Oh! I just had an idea. If I buy her some gum, she'll chew it and her breath will smell good!
Fran: Good idea! Now, what if I told you that *your* breath smells . . .
Scott: Hey!
Fran: Only joking!

Speaking Success!

Sentence fragments are incomplete sentences. They are common in speech but not in formal writing.

If you're not busy.
Really upset.
Not cool.
Good idea!
Over there.

2 Vocabulary

A. Write the correct vocabulary words under each picture.

sad excited bored scared nervous relieved suspicious

______

______

______

______

______

______

______

B. Work with a partner. Discuss a recent time when you felt each of these emotions.

Last week I saw a horror movie at home. I watched it alone, and I was so ***scared****!*

3 Essential Expressions

Look at the sentences below. Fill in the blanks with the following words.

relieved	sad	because	bored
weird	excited	before	

1. I was really nervous ______ my big interview, but I got the job!
2. Jenna is really ______ about her trip to South America.
3. He was acting ______, so I was a bit suspicious of him.
4. I really hate flying, so I am always ______ when the plane lands safely.
5. Tony almost ran out of the movie theater ______ he was so scared.
6. Maria was ______ to have to go home, but she had many great memories.
7. Paul was ______ because he was stuck at home.

4 Listening

A. Listen to Oscar and Rose talking about some unreal situations. Write a number next to each question in the order it is asked. Track 31

- ______ What if you woke up one morning and discovered you could speak English like a native speaker?
- ______ Suppose you were doing an exam and someone tried to copy your answers. What would you do?
- ______ If you could have any job in the world, what would you do?
- ______ What would you do if you woke up in the middle of the night and you saw a big spider on your bedroom wall?
- ______ You are at school. When you bend over to pick something up, your pants tear wide open in the back. What would you do?
- ______ What if you threw a baseball through your neighbor's window by mistake?

B. Listen again. Complete Rose's responses.

1. I would ________________, and then I would _________ somebody to kill it.
2. I would go to _________________________ to pay for the broken window.
3. I would _________________________ the teacher if I could change seats.
4. I would go to ________________.
5. I would be ________________ and travel to different places and ________________.
6. I would cry and then ________________ as fast as possible to change.

C. Work in a group. Discuss Rose's answers.

Rose would scream if she saw a spider at night. I would probably just go back to sleep . . .

5 Discussion

A. Get into small groups. Talk about the situations below.

What would you do if...

1
you found a job you really liked, but your parents wanted you to get a higher-paying job?

2
you found out that your 17-year-old sister was dating a 40-year-old man?

3
you borrowed your father's car secretly and got in an accident and smashed the car?

4
you really loved a person but your parents were against it?

5
your parents told you that you had to be home by 10:00 every night?

What does your group think? Write any interesting points below.

1. ______________________
2. ______________________
3. ______________________
4. ______________________
5. ______________________

B. Discuss these questions with your whole class. Your teacher will lead the discussion and write responses on the board.

6 Partner-Up

A. Talk about the following situations with a partner, and write his/her responses. First, think of two more situations.

1. If I were rich . . . ______________________
2. If I were married . . . ______________________
3. If I were a man/woman . . . ______________________
4. If I could fly . . . ______________________
5. If I didn't have to work . . . ______________________
6. If I didn't have a TV . . . ______________________
7. If I ______________ . . . ______________________
8. If I ______________ . . . ______________________

B. Work with your partner. Ask and answer the questions from page 80. Discuss each other's answers.

If I tore the back of my pants at school, then I would probably want to . . .

C. Choose one of the situations from this unit. Imagine that it came true. Write a diary entry to yourself about how you felt and what you did.

Use this as an example:

When I woke up last week, I discovered I could fly! It was amazing! I stepped out of the house and suddenly I flew up into the air. I flew all the way to school, and all the way home. On the weekend I decided to see how far I could fly. I flew all the way to South America! I think tomorrow I will . . .

D. Present your writing to the class.

Integrated Learning

1 Comprehension

A. **Read the questionnaire below. Answer the questions. If you answer "other," you must think of a unique answer.**

1. Imagine you were sitting on a train when an elderly woman got on. Would you:
   - ☐ get up and give her your seat?
   - ☐ pretend you were asleep?
   - ☐ other: ____________________

2. If a classmate asked to borrow your car to go skiing, would you:
   - ☐ let him borrow your car?
   - ☐ suggest that he take the train instead?
   - ☐ other: ____________________

3. What if you saw a foreigner who didn't know how to use the subway ticket machine? Would you:
   - ☐ wait for someone else to help her?
   - ☐ try to help her?
   - ☐ other: ____________________

4. Imagine you were going to the video store to rent a movie. On the way you saw a cute lost dog. Would you:
   - ☐ take him home with you?
   - ☐ continue on to the video store and forget the dog?
   - ☐ other: ____________________

5. Suppose that while you were in New York City on vacation, a homeless man walked up to you and asked for $5. Would you:
   - ☐ give the person the money?
   - ☐ refuse to give him money?
   - ☐ other: ____________________

6. If you were walking home from the station late at night and saw a drunk man lying in the middle of the road, would you:
   - ☐ help him get up?
   - ☐ ignore him and keep going?
   - ☐ other: ____________________

B. **Now, three different classmates these questions and note their responses.**

C. **Work in a group. Did most people give the first or second answer? Do you think people are generally good or bad?**

Practice

1 Dialog

A. Listen to the recording and write the missing words that you hear. Track 30

Scott: Fran, can I ________ you something? If you're not __________.

Fran: Sure, go ahead. I'm not doing __________ right now.

Scott: Well, what would happen if I told you **your breath smelled really bad**?

Fran: What would __________? Wait, **does my breath smell**, Scott? Is that what you're saying?

Scott: No, no! Actually, I know someone who really likes me, but **her breath stinks**.

Fran: Hmm . . . why ________ you just tell her that **her breath smells**?

Scott: I can't tell her that! If I did, she'd be upset! ________ upset.

Fran: Yeah. Not ________. You can't say that about someone, can you?

Scott: Oh! I just had an ________. If I buy her some **gum**, she'll **chew** it and **her breath will smell good**!

Fran: Good idea! Now, what if I told you that your **breath smells** . . .

Scott: Hey!

Fran: Only joking!

B. Look at the bolded words in the dialog above. With a partner, think of some new information to replace these words.

C. Practice the dialog using the new information.

2 Picture Description

Listen and choose the statement that best describes what you see in the picture. Track 32

1.

Ⓐ Ⓑ Ⓒ Ⓓ

2.

Ⓐ Ⓑ Ⓒ Ⓓ

3 Unscramble

Unscramble the sentences below.

1. won the / If I / I would / lottery, / world. / travel the

→ ______________________________

2. so I / went to / was hungry, / the store. / I

→ ______________________________

3. get much / so I / I didn't / sleep last / am tired this / night, / morning.

→ ______________________________

4. pass the / need to / If you / study harder. / test, you / want to

→ ______________________________

5. don't get / If I / I will be / a second / really upset. / interview,

→ ______________________________

Note Taking

Main Points	Detail

Summary

Brainstorming

Journal/Activity Writing

UNIT 09 Future Plans

Talking About:
Things that haven't happened yet

Warm-Up

What are your plans for this weekend?
Where do you see yourself in five years' time?

1 Model Dialog

Listen and practice the dialog with a partner. Track 33

Susie: Leon, are you up to anything next week? We have a week's vacation.

Leon: Oh, so we do. I hadn't really thought about it. Are you going to do anything?

Susie: Yeah, I've got plans. I'm going to go snowboarding with my boyfriend.

Leon: Oh, that's great! I'll probably just stay at home and play video games.

Susie: That doesn't sound very fun to me. Won't you get bored at all?

Leon: Oh, no. I'll love it, I know. It will be nice to relax for a little bit.

Susie: Well, while you're at home I'll be zooming down a mountain! Much better.

Leon: I'm sure you're going to have a great time. I will too, though. Don't worry.

Susie: Yeah, it'll be nice for you to get some rest. Anyway, I've got to go now. See you!

Leon: Me, too. I'm going to the movies now. Later!

Speaking Success!

There are numerous ways that we can say **goodbye** in casual speech.

See you (later)!

Later!

Catch you later

Bye!

2 Vocabulary

A. **Work with a partner. Make future sentences using the verbs below.**

go swimming | visit | be | help | answer | recommend | forget | work | arrive

*I will **help** you as much as I can.*

There are two ways to construct sentences using the simple future: ***will*** and ***be going to***. They have similar meanings, but there are subtle differences.

*I **will** make dinner tonight.* *He **is going to** take a vacation.*

Will is used to talk about something that the speaker will do willingly (or not), or that is not definite.

*I **will not [won't]** do your homework for you.* *I**'ll** probably just stay home.*

Be going to is used to talk about a person's definite plan for the future.

*They **are going to** see a movie tonight.* *She **is going to** meet us at 7:00 p.m.*

B. **Look at these pictures. Write the correct number next to each picture.**

1. I promise it won't happen again!
2. I'll have the pasta, please.
3. I'll give him the message.
4. I'll be home about 8:00.

3 Essential Expressions

Look at the sentences below. Fill in the blanks with the following words.

forget	be	help	recommend	answer

1. I hope that he will ________________ me for the new position.
2. You will receive a(n) ________________ by email within a week.
3. Please try not to ________________ our appointment this afternoon.
4. The exhibition will ________________ open until 8:00 p.m. today.
5. Nigel will be able to ________________ you with your homework when he gets home.

4 Listening

A. **Listen to Charlie being interviewed by Nancy. Does he answer "Yes" or "No"? Check the correct answer.** Track 34

Is Charlie going to . . .	Yes	No
1. . . . do homework?	☐	☐
2. . . . stay up?	☐	☐
3. . . . wash dishes?	☐	☐
4. . . . watch TV?	☐	☐
5. . . . eat out?	☐	☐
6. . . . do laundry?	☐	☐
7. . . . take it easy?	☐	☐
8. . . . go on vacation?	☐	☐
9. . . . get married?	☐	☐

B. **Listen again. Write down the extra information that Charlie gives for each question.**

1. ______________________________
2. ______________________________
3. ______________________________
4. ______________________________
5. ______________________________
6. ______________________________
7. ______________________________
8. ______________________________
9. ______________________________

C. **Talk with a partner about Charlie's plans.**

Charlie isn't going to do homework today, because . . .

5 Survey

A. **Ask the following questions to three classmates. Write their responses.**

Are you going to . . .	Name ____________	Name ____________	Name ____________
. . . do homework tonight?			
. . . stay up past midnight?			
. . . wash dishes tomorrow?			
. . . watch TV tomorrow night?			
. . . eat out the day after tomorrow?			
. . . do laundry this week?			
. . . take it easy next vacation?			
. . . go anywhere next summer vacation?			
. . . get married before you're 25?			

B. **Find someone else in your class. Ask him/her the questions below.**

Do you think . . .

1. . . . you'll be living in the same place five years from now?
2. . . . you'll have a big wedding when you get married?
3. . . . you'll have more than two children?
4. . . . you'll ever get divorced?
5. . . . you'll ever make 1 million dollars a year?
6. . . . you'll ever buy a house?
7. . . . you'll ever live abroad?
8. . . . a woman will become the prime minister or president of your country in your lifetime?
9. . . . your country will put a man on the moon in the next ten years?
10. . . . a cure for cancer will be discovered in the next five years?

↑ I hope so.
↓ I hope not.

↑ Definitely.
Probably.
I might.
I doubt it.
↓ Definitely not.

C. **Work in a group. Discuss your classmates' answers. Present your ideas to the class.**

Susan thinks that she won't be living in the same place five years from now . . .

6 Partner-Up

A. Work with a partner. Ask and answer the following questions. Write their responses.

1. What are you going to do after class today?
   ____
2. What time are you going to have dinner?
   ____
3. What are you going to have for dinner?
   ____
4. Who is going to come to your home for dinner?
   ____
5. What are you going to do after dinner?
   ____
6. What are you going to do tomorrow?
   ____
7. What are you going to do the day after tomorrow?
   ____
8. What are you going to do next vacation?
   ____
9. When are you going to graduate?
   ____
10. What are you going to do after you graduate?
   ____

B. Talk to someone else in your class. Tell him/her about your partner's future plans.

Andrew is going to do his homework after class today. He is going to have . . .

Integrated Learning

1 Comprehension

A. Read Juliet talking about her thoughts on the future.

The future? The future scares me. Right now I'm studying accounting at university, but I'm not sure if I'm going to be an accountant in the future. I only chose it because I'm good at math. I can only think as far as the weekend! I'm going to the movie theater with some friends that I haven't seen for a while. It's going to be a really fun day. But I can't tell you where I will be five or ten years from now. I will get married at some point, hopefully, and I want to have kids. I think I'm going to take each day as it comes and not plan for the future. Let's see what happens!

B. Read the passage again. Answer these questions. Use full sentences.

1. What is Juliet studying at university? ____________________
2. How far can Juliet think? ____________________
3. What scares her? ____________________
4. What job does she mention? ____________________
5. Is she sure if she will have this job in the future? ____________________
6. What will she do at some point? ____________________
7. Does Juliet want to have children? ____________________

C. Write about your own plans for the future. If you don't have any plans, explain why not.

____

____

____

D. Present your writing to the class. Answer any questions people may have.

When I am older, I think that I will . . .

Practice

1 Dialog

A. Listen to the recording and write the missing words that you hear. Track 33

Susie: Leon, are you up to ________ next week? We have a week's vacation.

Leon: Oh, so we do. I hadn't really ________ about it. Are you going to do anything?

Susie: Yeah, I've got ________. I'm going to **go snowboarding** with my **boyfriend**.

Leon: Oh, that's great! I'll ____________ just stay at home and play **video games**.

Susie: That doesn't ________ very fun to me. Won't you get bored at all?

Leon: Oh, no. I'll love it, I know. It will be nice to ________ for a little bit.

Susie: Well, while you're at home I'll be **zooming down a mountain**! ________ better.

Leon: I'm sure you're going to have a great time. I will too, though. Don't ________.

Susie: Yeah, it'll be nice for you to get some rest. Anyway, I've got to go now. See you!

Leon: Me, too. I'm going to **the movies** now. Later!

B. Look at the bolded words in the dialog above. With a partner, think of some new information to replace these words.

C. Practice the dialog using the new information.

2 Picture Description

Listen and choose the statement that best describes what you see in the picture. Track 35

1.

Ⓐ Ⓑ Ⓒ Ⓓ

2.

Ⓐ Ⓑ Ⓒ Ⓓ

3 Unscramble

Unscramble the sentences below.

1. going to / the racetrack / We are / this weekend.
   → ______________________________

2. traveling around / I will / this time / be / next week.
   → ______________________________

3. will be / due to / rail strikes. / The start / delayed / of the rally
   → ______________________________

4. will be giving / this morning / The president / the White House. / a statement / in
   → ______________________________

5. the movie / are being / Props from / this afternoon. / auctioned off
   → ______________________________

Note Taking

Main Points	Detail

Summary

Brainstorming

Journal/Activity Writing

How to Use Units 10-12

1. Preview the unit together as a class. Talk about the title of the unit, the pictures throughout the unit, and the title of the reading passage (if different from the unit title). Ask students what they know about the topic.

2. Have students answer the warm-up questions on their own, then ask volunteers to read their answers aloud to the class.

3. Review the **Before You Read** section together as a class. Ask students to think about the passage as they move through the unit.

4. Have students work independently through vocabulary, listening, and reading sections. You will need to play the listening audio track for them. Review vocabulary words and useful expressions together.

5. Ask students to work through the comprehension activity on their own. Let them know that the class will soon be having a discussion about the unit.

6. As a class, review and answer the discussion questions. Allow for some debate and conversation. Acknowledge alternative viewpoints with positive feedback. There might not be 100% agreement, which is OK.

7. Break students into smaller groups based on the direction on the unit's writing activity. For essays and stories, students work independently and then share their writing with the class. Open the floor for some questions and discussion of the writing. For other activities, students will be able to work more collaboratively. Small groups work together to complete their tasks and then present their findings to the class. They build conversation and listening skills as they participate in interviews and debates. Again, allow the class to ask questions of presenters as well as decide who wins debates.

By creating an open environment, students will be more comfortable participating in discussions and will take away more from the unit as they form their own ideas and opinions.

Unit 10

The Korean Push for English Education

Warm-Up

1. Do you think it is necessary for all Koreans to study English? Why or why not?
2. Has English been valuable for you, or would you prefer not to have learned it?

BEFORE YOU READ

These days, most students in South Korea study English. However, many of these students don't even plan on traveling or working in international companies. A lot of people argue that being able to speak English is an advantage, but there are others who disagree. Some Koreans don't like the influence that English is having on their culture. Others don't believe being able to speak English is a necessary skill for everyone.

Vocabulary Preview

Match each word with its correct definition.

1. missionary •	• a. extensive exposure to surroundings or language
2. erode •	• b. a part of a regular cycle of change
3. phase •	• c. words combining the Korean and English languages
4. Konglish •	• d. to destroy slowly
5. immersion •	• e. a member of a religious group sent to an area to teach

Vocabulary Practice

Fill in the blanks. Use the words from the box.

phase	Konglish	eroded	immersion	missionaries

1. Words like 'handphone' and 'bolpen' are examples of ____________________.

2. Over many years, the river ____________________ the sides of the mountains. Now there is a canyon.

3. Most young children go through a ____________________ where they say, "No!" to everything.

4. When Nina was younger, she went to a school run by Christian ____________________ from France.

5. The German program at that school is ____________________. No one speaks anything but German during school hours.

Listen carefully to the following conversation and complete the note-taking activity.

Scene: *Two students are talking about their experiences with English lessons.*

Pam

She goes to ____________ different ____________ academies.

Her parents want her ____________ ________ for graduate ____________.

She practiced ________________ in ____________, Canada.

Jim

His ____________ wants him to work for ________________________.

He might get promoted with ________________________.

USEFUL EXPRESSIONS

driving me nuts: making me feel crazy; making me lose my mind (slang)

Reading

Track 37

Is English Really Necessary?

The English language is a hot commodity in Korea these days. Celebrities and business people are learning English. Everywhere you look there are English schools. Much of the focus in these English schools is English **immersion**. It is big business for owners of English teaching schools. There is also much money to be made as an English teacher. But learning English is not just an educational or business trend.

English has become fashionable and hip. Clothing and pop music all demonstrate the popularity of English. Olympic athletes and international business people might need it. World Cup soccer players and world travelers probably need to know English as well. However, some people question whether English study is necessary for the average Korean.

For example, many businesses are strictly Korean-operated. No one speaks English at these businesses. A large number of Koreans do not travel, so it seems pointless and wasteful to spend money on learning English.

There are those that are concerned about the effects of English on the Korean language. Already there are many English words that have been added into the Korean language. "**Konglish**" is humorous on T-shirts. But in this case, it is not so funny to think that the Korean language itself might be **eroding**. Some worry that they are already losing so much of their culture. Since language is part of culture, then it may be threatened as well.

People argue that English is the future. Perhaps it is. English could also be another passing **phase**. Koreans might be learning Spanish in another generation. Or maybe Westerners will be eager to learn Korean.

Whatever happens, English is certainly a big hit. It is hard to believe that a language brought to Korea by **missionaries** is now so widespread. English has become the universal business language. Perhaps it is of no surprise that speaking English is a commodity in Korea now.

USEFUL EXPRESSIONS

hot commodity: a valuable product or service
English immersion: speaking and being spoken to only in English in order to learn the language
passing phase: something that might be popular now, but not later

Comprehension

Complete the following chart based on the information you heard in Listening and read in Reading.

<table>
<tr><th>Koreans need English if they . . .</th><th>Koreans don't need English if they . . .</th></tr>
<tr><td>. . . work for a(n) ______________________ company.</td><td rowspan="3">. . . ______________________ for a national ______________________.</td></tr>
<tr><td>. . . are ______________________ travelers.</td></tr>
<tr><td>. . . ______________________ abroad.</td></tr>
<tr><td>. . . are Olympic ______________________.</td><td rowspan="3">. . . don't plan to ______________________ internationally.</td></tr>
<tr><td>. . . are World ______________________ athletes.</td></tr>
<tr><td>. . . ______________________ celebrities.</td></tr>
</table>

Discussion

Read and consider the following questions. Discuss them with your class.

1. What will happen if the English language becomes less important in the future? Will all these lessons and academies be a waste of time? Why or why not?
2. If you could learn a language other than Korean and English, what would it be? Explain your choice.

Writing

Further Discussion

Each group will discuss one of the topics below. During discussions, someone from each group should be assigned to take notes on the lines below. After discussions, another person from each group can stand up to present their group's to the class.

Group One: The Origins of English in Korea

Dutch may have been the first European language to enter Korea, but it did not have a great impact on the nation or its people. American soldiers brought the English language with them during the Korean War, and it has been here ever since.
What Korean words are similar to English words? Do you think your relatives learned any English from the American soldiers when they first came? Why do you think English has had such a great impact on Korea and its people?

Group Two: The Current Impact of English in Korea

Korea's public education system cannot keep up with the great demand to learn English. This is why language schools in the form of private businesses (academies) are so popular. Some students even hire private tutors.
Do you think going to English academies is a good idea? Why or why not? Which is better, learning from a private tutor or an English academy? Why? How can the public education system get better at teaching English?

Group Three: The Future of English in Korea

English has been the universal language for well over 200 years. In fact, the use of English has continued to grow because of the Internet, television, and other mass media. Most people believe that its influence will not slow down. Koreans interested in international business, sports, or education should know English.
Do you think most people need to learn English these days? Why or why not? Where do you see English in your daily life? Do you think the influence of English will slow down?

Note Taking

Main Points	Detail

Summary

Brainstorming

Journal/Activity Writing

Unit

11 The Westernization of Korean Society

Warm-Up

1. What are some examples of the Westernization of Korea?
2. Do you think Korea is the only nation in Asia that is being westernized? Why or why not?

BEFORE YOU READ

Many people argue that South Korea is being westernized, but it is more complicated than that. The world is becoming more global, and more ideas are being shared freely as a result. It is true that Koreans now have more variety in their lives, but the opposite is also true. Korean products are for sale all around the world. It might be better if these changes occurred more slowly, but that doesn't seem likely to happen.

Vocabulary Preview

Match each word with its correct definition.

1. literacy •	• a. someone to put blame on
2. Belgian •	• b. the state of being able to read
3. scapegoat •	• c. a piece of equipment designed for a particular use or function
4. exaggeration •	• d. coming from the European country of Belgium
5. appliance •	• e. the act of overstating a detail

Vocabulary Practice

Choose the word or phrase that is similar in meaning to the one provided.

1. scapegoat
a. sheep b. thief c. victim d. hero

2. literacy
a. book b. education c. teacher d. student

3. appliance
a. dishes b. electricity c. device d. clothing

4. exaggeration
a. overstatement b. simplification c. decrease d. minimization

5. Belgian
a. from Bosnia b. from Belarus c. from Belgium d. from Bulgaria

Listen carefully to the following presentation and complete the note-taking activity.

Scene: *A student is presenting her report on the dangers of Westernization in Korea.*

Damage 	Result 
Family values are ________________.	________________ have gotten higher.
Korean food ________________ ________________.	Fast food ________________ ________________. Obesity, ________________ ________ disease are increasing.
Korean small businesses ________ ________.	________________ ________ will replace smaller ones.

USEFUL EXPRESSIONS

phase out: to be replaced by something else; to be no longer in use

Reading

Track 39

Korea in the Global Village

Some people argue that Korea is being westernized. This would mean that Western culture is taking over. This is an **exaggeration**. While it is easy to villainize Western governments, the claim that the West is conquering Korea is inaccurate. There are many problems in the world, and America is often the **scapegoat**.

Korea is not being westernized; it is being modernized. You might say it is being globalized. Korea has successfully joined the 21st century. The strength of the Korean economy speaks volumes. Korean people enjoy a high standard of living. **Literacy** is high and health care is advanced. Poverty, crime, and homelessness are low. No one can say that Korea is suffering.

Foreign goods and services do not harm Korea. In fact, they make it better! There is nothing wrong with competition. Korean companies are urged to make their products better. Stores offer more choices and lower prices.

Korea is no longer called the "Hermit Kingdom." It has become a part of the global village. Koreans have access to products from all over the world. A Korean grocery store might sell **Belgian** chocolate. There is wine from Chile and France. Koreans can dine at fine Italian restaurants. American music and television are popular. European fashions are popular as well. Korea has never had such variety! Likewise, other nations enjoy Korean imports. Korean home **appliances** are sold everywhere, and almost everyone owns a Korean cell phone! There are even Korean car factories all over North America.

Technology is not the only thing being exported. Korea also exports talent and culture. Korean athletes are recognized worldwide. Figure skater Yu-Na Kim trains in Canada. Soccer star Ji-Sung Park plays for Manchester United. Korean music is equally respected. The pop star, Rain, stars in big-budget Hollywood movies. The Wonder Girls recently toured America. This is hardly the Westernization of Korea. It sounds more like the Koreanization of the West!

USEFUL EXPRESSIONS

speaks volumes: gives a lot of information about something
global village: all of the world connected and sharing resources
big-budget: produced at great expense

Comprehension

Complete the following chart based on the information you heard in Listening and read in Reading.

Modernization of Korea	Koreanization of the West
• Food is changing. • Koreans have a ______________ of living. • Literacy is ______________ and ______________ is advanced. • Poverty, crime, and ______________ are low. • Businesses are changing—have more ______________. • More open to the West: - International items can be found in ______________ stores. - ______________ music is popular.	• Korean ______________ are sold everywhere. • Almost everyone owns a ______________ ______________. • Korean ______________ are all over North America. • Korean athletes and musicians on the world stage: - Yu-Na Kim trains in ______________. - Ji-Sung Park plays for ______________ ______________. - Rain is in ______________. - The ______________ toured America.

Discussion

Read and consider the following questions. Discuss them with your class.

1. Are Western nations, like the United States, taking advantage of Korea? Or is it a fair exchange? Why?
2. Do you think Korean people could stop Westernization from happening if they wanted to? If so, how?

Writing Debate

Divide into teams of two and choose your topic. Write your arguments on the lines below. You will argue that the changes in Korean society are positive, or that the changes in Korean society are negative. Present your arguments in front of the class. Each team will have three opportunities to speak. The class will decide whose arguments were most convincing.

Team: ____________________

Things to Think About

What changes are positive/negative?
What is happening to some of the traditions?
How can the negative changes be switched to positive changes?
What are some of the damages and results?
How are family values changing?
How has the economy changed?

Argument One: ____________________

Argument Two: ____________________

Argument Three: ____________________

Note Taking

Main Points	Detail

Summary

Brainstorming

Journal/Activity Writing

Unit 12

A Developed Korea

Warm-Up

1. What do you think of when you hear that a country is "developed"? What are some developed countries?
2. What are some ways that Korea has changed since your grandparents were your age?

BEFORE YOU READ

South Korea has grown quickly, and so has its economy. It changed from an agricultural country to an industrial one in a very short amount of time. Because of this, the environment and some people have suffered. There isn't enough space, pollution is bad, and the division between rich and poor has increased. Koreans must now figure out how to fix their problems before they get any worse.

Vocabulary Preview

Match each word with its correct definition.

1. overwhelmed •	• a. capable of being continued in a way that does not damage those resources for future use
2. portion •	• b. intense or extreme
3. furious •	• c. completely defeated
4. sewage •	• d. human waste water
5. sustainable •	• e. a part

Vocabulary Practice

Choose the word or phrase that is similar in meaning to the one provided.

1. sustainable
a. finished　b. never ending　c. new　d. started

2. portion
a. piece　b. all　c. share　d. cut

3. overwhelmed
a. surprised　b. excited　c. flooded　d. grateful

4. sewage
a. clean water　b. garbage　c. dirty dishes　d. dirt

5. furious
a. calm　b. slow　c. wild　d. boring

Track 40

Listening

Listen carefully to the following lecture and complete the note-taking activity.

Scene: *A professor speaking to his class, reviewing a previous lecture.*

Early 1900s

- Korea was one of the ______________________ in the world.
- The ______________________ was bad.

1960 and After

- Industry and ______________________ replaced ______________________.
- The standard ______________________ improved.
- The gap between the ______________________ increased.
- There were about ______________________ registered cars.

1970s

About ______________________ of Koreans lived ______________________.

1999

There were about ______________________ registered cars.

2000

About ______________________ of Koreans lived ______________________.

USEFUL EXPRESSIONS

standard of living: the level of material comfort measured by goods, services, and luxuries available
urban center: large city; metropolitan area

Reading

Track 41

A Developed Korea: Looking to the Future

Industry and development in Korea have been a fast and **furious** series of events. Beginning after the Korean War, Koreans have pushed hard to make their nation a success. The fast pace of this development has created a few problems.

As in many parts of the world, pollution is a serious issue. Many early industrial projects were built quickly, without concern for the environment. Polluted air and water are some of the effects of these projects. Also, about 80% of all Koreans live in cities. As a result, there is great overcrowding of both people and cars. Services like **sewage** and public transportation are often **overwhelmed**, which adds to the pollution.

In addition, Koreans are running out of space! A large **portion** of the population wants to live in bigger houses. However, Korea is not a large country. There is only so much room to go around.

Pollution might be prevented or cleaned up, but not quickly. Factories cannot be stopped because Korea's economy depends on them. Cities will always be popular places to live in. Some land can be used for building, but not much. There are just no simple solutions.

Thankfully, steps are being taken. Korea, Japan, and China have been working together to deal with cross-border pollution. In 2008, the Korean government decided to invest in renewable energy. Solar power, wind power, and bio-fuels pollute the environment less than fossil fuels. Korea also has cutting-edge technology when it comes to electric cars. The good news is that all of these technological advances could allow Korea to keep its economy strong. New city planning and cleaner energy are becoming more common, as well.

Perhaps in the future, Korea can lead the world with new **sustainable** technology. That would be just another example of Koreans working hard to make their nation a success.

USEFUL EXPRESSIONS

renewable energy: energy that can be used over and over again

cutting-edge: the best or newest

Comprehension

Complete the following chart based on the information you heard in Listening and read in Reading.

Problems	Solutions
Pollution • ______________________ • water	**Renewable Energy** • solar ______________________ • ______________________ • ______________________
Overcrowding • ______________________ • ______________________	**New City** ____________
Overwhelmed Services • ______________________ • ______________________	

Discussion

Read and consider the following questions. Discuss them with your class.

1. Why do you think so many people want to live in cities, instead of living as fishermen or farmers? How would you prefer to live?
2. Why are China and Japan working together with Korea to deal with pollution?

Essay

Below are some facts pertaining to Korean wildlife. After reading through them, answer the questions to complete two paragraphs on the lines below. State your opinions. Use the questions as a guide, and add details wherever appropriate. Be prepared to read your paragraphs in class.

Things to Think About

- As a "bridge" between north and south Asia, Korea is important for migrating birds. Wetlands and coastal areas are especially important – and these are areas most commonly used for industrial and urban development.
- Many of Korea's rivers are being made into shipping canals, which will make them uninhabitable for wildlife.
- Korea used to be home to many tigers and bears. Sadly, the last tigers became extinct in the 1920s. Some bears still live in the Jiri and Seorak mountain ranges. Deer, wild pigs, and smaller mammals can be seen in a few places, but their territories and populations are shrinking.
- The Demilitarized Zone (DMZ) between North and South Korea has become a rare and valuable "nature park." World experts are interested in the animals and birds that have been living there, undisturbed by human beings, for over 50 years.
- Popular Korean hobbies, like photography and hiking, can make a difference. Public awareness and education can help to save Korea's wild forests and animals.

Which is more important: industry and urban development or saving wildlife? Why? Do you think most Koreans agree with you? How do you think pollution and overcrowding in Korea has affected Korea's wild animals? How do you think renewable energy and city planning can help save wildlife? Give an example.

Note Taking

Main Points	Detail

Summary

Brainstorming

Journal/Activity Writing

Appendix

Appendix I

UNIT 01 Daily Life

Work with a partner. Partner B looks at this page, and Partner A looks at page 12. Tell your partner what you did yesterday.

I woke up at 6:30. Then I had a shower. After that I . . .

Partner B

1

2

3

4

5

6

After school

7

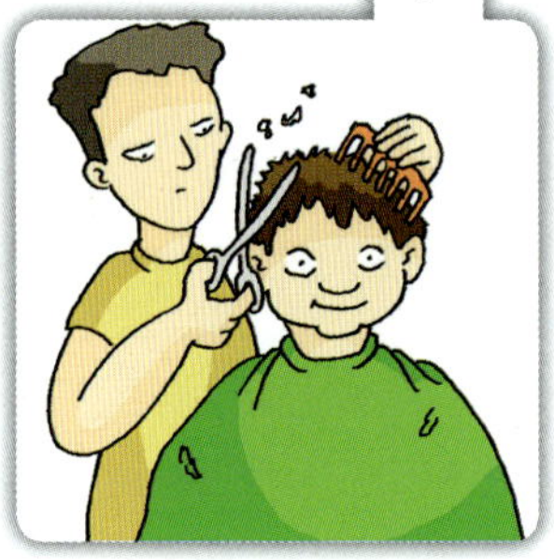

8

9

In the afternoon

10

After dinner

11

In the evening

12

UNIT 05 Around the World

Work with a partner. Look at the cards on this page. Follow the directions on page 52 to play the game.

CANADA

BRAZIL

THAILAND

INDIA

THE PHILIPPINES

AUSTRALIA

MEXICO

CHINA

FRANCE

RUSSIA

COLOMBIA

EGYPT

NEW ZEALAND

SOUTH AFRICA

TAIWAN

USA

SPAIN

SOUTH KOREA

GERMANY

ENGLAND

ITALY

JAPAN

INDONESIA

MALAYSIA

VIETNAM

Listening Transcripts

Unit 01 Daily Life

Track 1

Veronica: Patrick, you look tired today. What time did you go to bed last night?
Patrick: Hi Veronica, what's up? Yeah, I'm pretty sleepy. I got to bed around 3:00 a.m.
Veronica: Three in the morning? Wow, that's late. Did you go out last night?
Patrick: No, I was studying for this big test next week.
Veronica: Oh, so you were up all night studying? That's too bad.
Patrick: Yeah, I was drinking coffee and energy drinks to stay awake.
Veronica: Oh, my. That's not good for you, you know. Coffee makes me sick.
Patrick: Yeah, I regret it now. I missed my first class this morning, actually!
Veronica: I always set my alarm for 7:00 a.m. so I can get to class early.
Patrick: Well, you're a better student than me!

Track 2

1. listened to music
2. drove
3. played tennis
4. went shopping
5. washed dishes
6. slept
7. watched TV
8. met friends

Track 3

Woman: Brian, why were you peeping in your neighbor's window at 4:00 a.m. last night?
Brian: I wasn't peeping. I just . . . I saw a light and I wondered what it was. I wanted to check that no one was breaking in, so I went across to have a look. But it turns out it was just their son, and he was just getting something to eat.
Woman: Oh. OK.
Brian: Yeah.
Woman: Why were you shouting at the pilot while you were flying to Europe?
Brian: I'm really afraid of flying, and when the plane started turning I thought we were going to crash . . .
Woman: Wow!
Brian: So, I wanted to ask the pilot if everything was OK.
Woman: Wow—you looked really crazy!
Brian: I was scared.
Woman: OK. Why were you walking down the street carrying a snake and chair?
Brian: Because I'm in a play and the play needed the props, and the props were the snake and the chair.
Woman: Why were you sitting on the side of the road crying?
Brian: Because my girlfriend just broke up with me, and I really liked her.
Woman: Oh, that's too bad. I'm sorry. Why were you wearing a Boy Scout uniform at work?
Brian: Because it's Halloween, and everyone dresses up on Halloween.
Woman: Oh. You looked very good in it. Very nice.
Brian: Thank you.
Woman: Why were you lying on top of a table at the fast-food restaurant?
Brian: Because I felt really sick after eating my meal, and needed to lie down.

Track 4

1. **A.** Children are playing outside the school.
B. The school building is closed for the day.
C. The school probably has many playgrounds.
D. Students are walking in front of the school.

2. **A.** The students are talking to each other.
B. The students are taking an exam.
C. The class has just been dismissed.
D. The students are sitting in their desks.

Unit 02 Giving Directions

Track 5

Sara: Excuse me, sir. Could you help me, please? I'm a little lost.
Policeman: Of course. Where do you need to go, ma'am?
Sara: Well, I've been trying to find the Sea View Shopping Arcade for the last hour!
Policeman: OK. Let me help you. Go straight up this road until you reach the intersection.
Sara: Pardon me? I couldn't hear you.
Policeman: Walk up the road to the intersection. Then go straight until you see the bank.
Sara: Up the intersection, walk until I see the bank, right.
Policeman: Yep. The arcade is across from the bank. You can't miss it.
Sara: Thank you very much. You've been very helpful. I'm sure I'll find it now.

Policeman: My pleasure. Enjoy your shopping, ma'am.

Track 6

1. **Man:** Uh . . . excuse me, ma'am.
Woman: Yes.
Man: Uh . . . could you tell me how to get to the City Hospital?
Woman: Let's see . . . the City Hospital? OK—you want to take this road straight for two blocks.
Man: OK.
Woman: And then take a left. Walk past the Star Hotel, and the City Hospital will be on your right-hand side.
Man: Thank you very much.
Woman: No problem.

2. **Woman:** Excuse me, sir.
Man: Yes?
Woman: Uh . . . could you give me directions to the Food Bag Family Diner?
Man: Hmm . . . the Food Bag . . . OK—you're going to go up this street two blocks . . .
Woman: OK.
Man: . . . and turn right. OK?
Woman: All right.
Man: Go straight for two more blocks, and the Food Bag Family Diner is on your left, at the intersection of First Avenue and Pearl Street.
Woman: Great! Thank you very much.
Man: No problem.

3. **Woman:** Excuse me.
Man: Hi.
Woman: Can you tell me how to get to the Washington Hotel?
Man: The Washington Hotel. Sure. All right—what you want to do is take your first left, walk straight a little way, and the Washington Hotel is on your left.
Woman: Oh, OK. So it'll be on my left?
Man: Right. Exactly.
Woman: OK. Thank you.
Man: You're welcome.

4. **Man:** Sorry, ma'am.
Woman: Yes?
Man: Can you . . . can you tell me how to get to Ace Rental Car?
Woman: Ace Rental Car? Sure. OK—what you want to do is go up this street for one block and make a right onto Second Avenue.
Man: Uh-huh.
Woman: Before you get to the next junction, Ace Rental Car will be on your right.
Man: On my right?
Woman: Yes.
Man: OK. Thank you.
Woman: You're welcome.

Track 7

Joanne: Excuse me. Is there a grocery store near here?
Stranger: Yes, there is Farmer Tom's Fruits.
Joanne: Oh, good. Do you know the way?
Stranger: Sure. Go straight ahead and turn left onto North Street.
Joanne: North Street, got it.
Stranger: Go straight until you see the church.
Joanne: OK. And the grocery store is there?
Stranger: The grocery store is behind the church.
Joanne: Thank you so much.
Stranger: That's OK. Hurry, it'll close soon!

Track 8

1. **A.** His point was lost.
B. The police car is parked.
C. The policeman is helping someone.
D. The policeman is arresting a man.
2. **A.** The cars are parked in front of the building.
B. They're walking in the park.
C. The joggers are chasing a car.
D. The building is on a corner.

Unit 03 Sickness & Health

Track 9

Ellie: Trevor, how are you doing? I haven't seen you for a while.
Trevor: Hey, Ellie. Yeah, I've been really sick for the last few days.
Ellie: Oh, no, are you OK? I heard there was a virus going around. My mom was sick.
Trevor: I guess I had that. I had a headache, a runny nose, and a bad stomach.
Ellie: Oh, that's horrible. Are you feeling better now?
Trevor: A little bit. I have an exam today, so I had to come in.
Ellie: If you feel really sick, just tell your teacher. I'm sure she'll understand.

Trevor: She won't. My teacher is Miss Anderton. She hates sick people.
Ellie: I know her. She's super-fit, isn't she? She exercises every day.
Trevor: And she's never sick. She'll say it's my fault! It's so unfair!

Track 10

Woman: Do you smoke more than three cigarettes a day?
Dean: Yes. Yes, I do.
Woman: Do you get drunk once or more per month?
Dean: Yes. Yes, I do.
Woman: Do you eat junk food almost every day?
Dean: Yes, I do.
Woman: Uh–huh. Do you usually get enough sleep?
Dean: Yes, I've been getting a lot of sleep recently.
Woman: Do you need to lose weight?
Dean: I don't think so.
Woman: Do you catch a cold more than twice a year?
Dean: No.
Woman: No?
Dean: No, I don't.
Woman: Do you have your teeth cleaned once a year?
Dean: Yes, I do.
Woman: Do you eat fruits and vegetables almost every day?
Dean: Yes, I do.
Woman: Do you exercise at least three times a week?
Dean: Certainly.
Woman: Uh-huh. Is work or school stressful for you?
Dean: Oh, very much so.
Woman: School's stressful?
Dean: School is very stressful.

Track 11

Man: How often do you get a cold?
Hayley: This year, I've had a cold three times. But, usually only maybe once a year.
Man: How often do you get a headache?
Hayley: I get a lot of headaches. I get headaches every week.
Man: When was the last time that you had the flu?
Hayley: The last time I had the flu was last year.
Man: Do you have any allergies?
Hayley: No, I don't have any allergies.
Man: Have you ever been in the hospital?
Hayley: Yes, but only one time.
Man: Why were you in the hospital?
Hayley: I had suspected malaria. I was really sick.
Man: OK . . . let's move on. What's something that makes you feel nauseous?
Hayley: Certain foods like seafood. Shellfish makes me feel nauseous.
Man: What's something that makes you feel dizzy?
Hayley: I feel really dizzy when we go really fast in my car.

Track 12

1. **A.** The boy is looking through a telescope.
   B. The doctor is asking the boy questions.
   C. The doctor is checking the boy's eyes.
   D. They're rearranging the office.
2. **A.** They're using some medical equipment.
   B. The doctor is teaching a class.
   C. The nurses are standing by.
   D. They're putting away medical supplies.

Unit 04 Cooking

Track 13

Louis: Good morning. Mmm . . . something smells good!
Leslie: Yeah, I'm frying some bacon and making scrambled eggs.
Louis: Oh, yummy! I love bacon, but I don't know how to make scrambled eggs.
Leslie: You don't know? I'll teach you! Crack a few eggs into a bowl, and add some milk.
Louis: Got it. Then whisk the eggs together, right?
Leslie: That's right. Beat them until the yolk and the white are mixed together.
Louis: And then I guess I need some seasoning, don't I?
Leslie: Yes! Add in some salt and pepper. I think you know how to do this.
Louis: Well, I've watched my dad do it a few times. I guess I picked it up.
Leslie: Then add some butter to a heated pan and pour in the mixture. Delicious!

Track 14

1. This is a fruit and it's kind of sour. It's bigger than an orange, and it's pink inside.
2. This is sweet and made by bees. And it's sticky.
3. This is a white liquid that you might drink or put on a bowl of cereal.
4. This is sweet white stuff that you can bake with, or put in a cup of coffee to make it sweeter.
5. This is a kind of frozen dessert that comes in a lot of flavors, and you can eat it on a cone or in a dish, and maybe put chocolate syrup on top.
6. This is a white-colored powdery substance used in baking. It is . . . comes in whole wheat or white.
7. This is a type of fruit that you can find in Hawaii. It has a very thick shell, but whenever you crack it open, it has milk inside.
8. This is a fruit. It's a dried grape. And it's dark brown.
9. This a creamy yellow substance. You spread it on toast.
10. This is usually eaten at the movies. Most people like to add butter and salt to it. It's very light.
11. This is a snack food. It's very salty and crunchy. It usually comes in a bag.
12. It's made from fermented milk. It's very creamy, and it's healthy.

Track 15

1. grapefruit	**2.** honey
3. milk	**4.** sugar
5. ice cream	**6.** flour
7. coconut	**8.** raisin
9. butter	**10.** popcorn
11. potato chips	**12.** yogurt

Track 16

1. **A.** The man is baking a cake.
   B. The man is reading an online recipe.
   C. The man is sending a message.
   D. The man is chatting on the Internet.
2. **A.** A man is eating vegetables.
   B. A man is cutting bananas.
   C. A man is preparing ingredients.
   D. A man has cut his finger.

Unit 05 Around the World

Track 17

Gemma: Muhammad, how are you doing? You look excited.
Muhammad: Oh, I am! Very! Today is Eid. It's my favorite day of the year.
Gemma: Eid? What's that? Is it like Christmas?
Muhammad: Well, it's a Muslim holiday, to celebrate the end of Ramadan.
Gemma: Oh, yes. Ramadan is when you fast during the day, isn't it?
Muhammad: Yes, it's like Lent for Christians. So, Eid is like Easter, I guess.
Gemma: Do you eat a lot of delicious food? And play music?
Muhammad: Yes, we have a huge feast, and we party and celebrate all day.
Gemma: That sounds like a lot of fun! I wish I could go!
Muhammad: Oh, why don't you join me? My mother always makes too much food.
Gemma: No, I couldn't. I didn't fast, so it's not for me! Have fun, though!
Muhammad: Thanks! See you later, Gemma.

Track 18

1. Japanese	**2.** German
3. Chinese	**4.** Australian
5. Taiwanese	**6.** Russian
7. American	**8.** Spanish
9. New Zealander	**10.** Brazilian
11. Mexican	**12.** English

Track 19

Man: Rebecca, do you like Mexican food?
Rebecca: Love it! Love Mexican food. It's so good. It's my favorite.
Man: What kind of Mexican food can you make?
Rebecca: Oh, my goodness. Well, tacos are pretty easy to make. Umm . . . and then, of course, nachos are easy because you just kind of throw in the cheese and the salsa and melt it. That's all I can make!
Man: Do you like Chinese food?
Rebecca: Love it! I lived in China for a year and I ate it all the time.
Man: What kind of Chinese food can you make?
Rebecca: See, I can't really make this food, but I

love wonton soup.

Man: What's that?

Rebecca: It's got dumplings in it and noodles. It's really good.

Man: OK. Umm . . . do you like Italian food?

Rebecca: Oh, I love it.

Man: What kind of Italian food can you make?

Rebecca: Hmm . . . well, I can make pasta, and I make a pretty good pizza, too.

Man: Do you like Indian food?

Rebecca: I don't believe I've ever had Indian food.

Man: OK. So then I guess you've never really made Indian food, then.

Rebecca: No.

Man: Do you like Korean food?

Rebecca: I can't say that I've ever had Korean food.

Man: Do you like Thai food?

Rebecca: Yes. I like everything, really!

Track 20

Partner A

1. Germany
2. Italy
3. Chinese and English
4. Asia
5. Mandarin Chinese
6. Indonesia
7. Portuguese

Partner B

1. Thailand
2. New Zealand
3. India
4. Mexico City
5. Greenland
6. South Korea
7. Australia, Canada, New Zealand, the USA, Hong Kong, Singapore, Taiwan

Track 21

1. **A.** The artwork shows the president making a speech.
   B. The artwork shows an angel blowing a horn.
   C. The tour guide is explaining the statue.
   D. They're taking pictures of the statue.
2. **A.** A breeze is blowing the flags.
   B. There are three flags in front of the hotel.
   C. The flags are being replaced.
   D. The hotel is near the water.

Unit 06 Telling Stories

Track 22

Josh: Did you have a good weekend, Cheryl? You went to the beach, right?

Cheryl: Well, I was going to go with my sisters. But the weather was awful.

Josh: Yeah, it was. Did you do something else instead?

Cheryl: Yes, we had traveled all the way to the beach, so we went to the Sea View Arcade.

Josh: That's a shopping center, isn't it?

Cheryl: Yep, it's huge. We spent ages looking at the sales, and we each got a manicure.

Josh: That sounds nice. My weekend was terrible.

Cheryl: Oh, really? How so?

Josh: I got stood up on a blind date. Then I was late to work on Sunday, and I got fired!

Cheryl: Oh, no! Did your alarm clock not go off?

Josh: Yeah, I think the batteries died. Well, I'm off to look for a new job!

Track 23

1. visited	**2.** promised
3. moved	**4.** played
5. performed	**6.** laughed
7. walked	**8.** brushed
9. showed	**10.** cried
11. graduated	**12.** liked

Track 24

Woman: Did you get up before 9:00 yesterday?

Lewis: Yesterday? Yesterday was Sunday. No, I didn't! I got up at 1:00 in the afternoon.

Woman: Did you eat breakfast?

Lewis: No . . . I never eat breakfast.

Woman: Did you check your email?

Lewis: Yep. I always check my email, every day.

Woman: Did you do laundry?

Lewis: Oh . . . no, I didn't. My mom does my laundry.

Woman: Did you wash your car?

Lewis: Yes, I did!

Woman: Did you work out at the gym?

Lewis: Yeah, I was at the gym for over three hours. I had a really good workout.

Woman: Did you play basketball?

Lewis: No, I didn't. I was too tired after working

	out at the gym.
Woman:	Did you go shopping?
Lewis:	Yes, I did. I bought a birthday present for my girlfriend.
Woman:	Did you go see a movie?
Lewis:	No, I didn't.
Woman:	Did you go to bed before midnight?
Lewis:	Yes, I did—because I had to get up really early this morning to go to work.

Track 25

1. **A.** Strangers are making small talk at a bus stop.
   B. The men are helping the women carry their bags.
   C. Friends are laughing and talking on the street.
   D. The women are assisting the men.
2. **A.** The sheep are moving ahead of the shepherd.
   B. The sheep are eating grass.
   C. There are a lot of wolves behind the sheep.
   D. The sheep are chasing the dog.

Unit 07 Eating Out

Track 26

Melody:	Are you hungry, Billy? I'm absolutely starving!
Billy:	Yeah, me, too. But I don't think we have anything in the fridge.
Melody:	How about if we go out? There's a new Chinese place round the corner.
Billy:	Chinese? Hmm . . . how about Indian food?
Melody:	Indian food? Oh no, I can't eat that. It's much too spicy for me!
Billy:	They have lots of other stuff, too. The waiters there are very helpful.
Melody:	How about something else? Pizza, maybe?
Billy:	We had pizza yesterday! I want Indian food.
Melody:	Well, I want Chinese! Let's both go and buy takeout, and eat it back here.
Billy:	Sure! I prefer eating at home to eating out, actually.
Melody:	Yeah, this way we can eat at home, but there are no dishes to wash. Let's go!
Billy:	Great!

Track 27

Dennis:	What kind of restaurants do you usually go to?
Anna:	When I eat out, I usually go to Thai restaurants. It's my favorite.
Dennis:	Mmm . . . I like Thai, too. What's a restaurant you like that isn't very well-known?
Anna:	Hmm . . . I really like BBQ House.
Dennis:	BBQ House?
Anna:	Yeah.
Dennis:	What kind of food do they have?
Anna:	They have a lot of barbecue food.
Dennis:	Is it . . . is it expensive?
Anna:	Not at all. It's very cheap.
Dennis:	Oh, good.
Anna:	Umm . . . and it's really interesting. It's like "Texasy," sort of. It's a really nice casual atmosphere.
Dennis:	Casual atmosphere? So, you wouldn't have to dress up for it?
Anna:	Not at all.
Dennis:	Oh, good. I like those kinds of restaurants. What beverage do you usually order when you go out for dinner?
Anna:	I usually just get water.
Dennis:	When you order a salad, what kind of dressing do you usually get?
Anna:	Sometimes I get ranch, but usually I get French dressing.
Dennis:	Oh, I like ranch. What's a dessert you often order?
Anna:	When I order dessert, which isn't very often, I get chocolate cake.
Dennis:	Mmm . . . that's delicious! Do you usually pay cash or use a credit card when you eat out?
Anna:	Oh, I don't like credit cards, so I always use cash.
Dennis:	Ah . . . do you always leave a fifteen-percent tip?
Anna:	I'm a waitress, so I . . . I leave more than a fifteen-percent tip—like twenty to twenty-five.
Dennis:	That's really good of you.

Track 28

Front Desk:	Good evening, this is Keo's. May I help you?
Customer:	Yes, I'd like to reserve a table for this Friday at 7:00.
Front Desk:	Certainly. For how many?
Customer:	For three people.
Front Desk:	OK. Would you like smoking or non-

	smoking?
Customer:	Non-smoking, please.
Front Desk:	And could I have your name, please?
Customer:	My name's Bill Swanson.
Front Desk:	Thank you, Mr. Swanson. I've reserved a table for three on Friday at 7:00.
Customer:	Thank you. Goodbye.
Front Desk:	Goodbye, see you on Friday!

Track 29

1. **A.** The man is having a drink with friends.
   B. The man is filling his glass with water.
   C. The man is putting food on his dish.
   D. The man is spilling water on the table.
2. **A.** The beach is very crowded.
   B. The terrace is full of tables and chairs.
   C. The server is explaining the menu to the customers.
   D. The umbrellas are leaning on the tables.

Unit 08 Unreal Situations

Track 30

Scott:	Fran, can I ask you something? If you're not busy.
Fran:	Sure, go ahead. I'm not doing anything right now.
Scott:	Well, what would happen if I told you your breath smelled really bad?
Fran:	What would happen? Wait, does my breath smell, Scott? Is that what you're saying?
Scott:	No, no! Actually, I know someone who really likes me, but her breath stinks.
Fran:	Hmm . . . why don't you just tell her that her breath smells?
Scott:	I can't tell her that! If I did, she'd be upset! Really upset.
Fran:	Yeah. Not cool. You can't say that about someone, can you?
Scott:	Oh! I just had an idea. If I buy her some gum, she'll chew it and her breath will smell good!
Fran:	Good idea! Now, what if I told you that *your* breath smells . . .
Scott:	Hey!
Fran:	Only joking!

Track 31

Oscar:	What would you do if you woke up in the middle of the night and you saw a big spider on your bedroom wall?
Rose:	I would scream so loudly, and then I would go and find somebody to kill it.
Oscar:	What if you threw a baseball through your neighbor's window by mistake?
Rose:	I would go to my neighbor and offer to pay for the broken window.
Oscar:	Very noble of you. Suppose you were doing an exam and someone tried to copy your answers. What would you do?
Rose:	I would raise my hand and ask the teacher if I could change seats.
Oscar:	What if you woke up one morning and discovered you could speak English like a native speaker?
Rose:	I would go to Australia.
Oscar:	If you could have any job in the world, what would you do?
Rose:	I would be a travel photographer and travel to different places and take pictures.
Oscar:	You are at school. When you bend over to pick something up, your pants tear wide open in the back. What would you do?
Rose:	I would cry and then hurry back to my dorm as fast as possible to change.

Track 32

1. **A.** The room has two stairs.
   B. There is a spiral staircase in the room.
   C. There are stairs leading to the wall.
   D. The room is an office with a desk.
2. **A.** These people are enjoying their coffee.
   B. The people are sitting and smiling at a table.
   C. The people are arguing with each other.
   D. The people are talking to each other outside.

Unit 09 Future Plans

Track 33

Susie:	Leon, are you up to anything next week? We have a week's vacation.
Leon:	Oh, so we do. I hadn't really thought about it. Are you going to do anything?
Susie:	Yeah, I've got plans. I'm going to go snowboarding with my boyfriend.
Leon:	Oh, that's great! I'll probably just stay at home and play video games.

Susie: That doesn't sound very fun to me. Won't you get bored at all?
Leon: Oh, no. I'll love it, I know. It will be nice to relax for a little bit.
Susie: Well, while you're at home I'll be zooming down a mountain! Much better.
Leon: I'm sure you're going to have a great time. I will too, though. Don't worry.
Susie: Yeah, it'll be nice for you to get some rest. Anyway, I've got to go now. See you!
Leon: Me, too. I'm going to the movies now. Later!

Track 34

Nancy: Are you going to do homework tonight?
Charlie: Nope. Today is Saturday—no homework.
Nancy: Are you going to stay up past midnight?
Charlie: Yes—it's Saturday!
Nancy: Are you going to wash dishes tomorrow?
Charlie: No. I'm going to go to the cafeteria. They are going to wash my dishes for me!
Nancy: Are you going to watch TV tomorrow night?
Charlie: No, I don't have a TV.
Nancy: Are you going to eat out the day after tomorrow?
Charlie: Umm . . . probably not. I need to save money.
Nancy: Are you going to do laundry this week?
Charlie: Yes. I haven't done it for a month!
Nancy: OK. Are you going to take it easy next vacation?
Charlie: Yeah—that's what vacations are for.
Nancy: Are you going to go anywhere next vacation?
Charlie: Yes. I'm going to visit my cousin.
Nancy: Hmm . . . are you going to get married before you're twenty-five?
Charlie: No! I don't want to get married.

Track 35

1. **A.** The office workers are discussing their vacation plans.
   B. The men are discussing their concert.
   C. The men with hardhats are looking at some plans.
   D. The businessman is lost.
2. **A.** The couple is sitting at their desks.
   B. They are relaxing in the park.
   C. The couple is sitting on the floor.
   D. The paper is behind the couple.

UNIT 10 The Korean Push for English Education

Track 36

Woman: My English homework is driving me nuts!
Man: What's the problem?
Woman: Well, there's so much vocabulary to learn, for one thing!
Man: Oh, you must go to one of those academies. Is it one where you have to memorize a hundred new words every week?
Woman: It feels more like a thousand! But that's only one academy. I go to two.
Man: Two different English academies? Wow!
Woman: Yeah, my parents are pretty strict. They want me to go to Harvard for graduate school, so my test scores have to be perfect.
Man: I hear you. My parents are like that, too. But we're actually very lucky, if you think about it.
Woman: That's true! Last summer I was in Vancouver, and I learned how valuable these English lessons really are.
Man: Did you have a chance to practice with Canadians?
Woman: Plenty! I ordered at restaurants, I took taxis, I even asked people for directions. I kept thinking that all those nights of studying and memorizing were finally paying off!
Man: That's good to hear. My father is trying to get me into a junior management position at his company. He thinks that with better English skills, I can easily get promoted.
Woman: Good for you! They might even send you on business trips to Canada! Or Australia!
Man: Or Hawaii!
Woman: Sounds like a great job, if you ask me!

UNIT 11 The Westernization of Korean Society

Track 38

My report is called "The Westernization of Korea."
We are witnessing the strongest economic growth that Korea has ever seen. Korean industry and business have never been more successful. Everything is great, right? You might be wondering why I would criticize the Westernization of Korea.
I believe that Westernization is doing a lot of damage.

Traditions that worked for hundreds of years have been thrown out. The family values that have always kept communities intact are disappearing. As a result, there are now higher crime rates in Korea.

Korean food that kept people healthy and strong for many generations is being phased out. Fast food restaurants are threatening Korean people's health and well-being. Obesity, diabetes, and heart disease will soon be a common part of Korean society.

Many Korean companies are small and new compared to their Western counterparts. They haven't had time to develop. But now, they have to compete with everyone else. Many Korean businesses will fail or be replaced by bigger and better foreign businesses.

I don't want to say everything is terrible. Western nations have also contributed a great deal to Korea. But perhaps some things are happening too quickly. Everyone is excited about change, but no one is taking the time to stop and think about it.

Thank you for listening.

Unit 12 A Developed Korea

Track 40

Early in the 20th century, Korea was one of the poorest countries in the world. The economy was bad, and there were many poor and unhealthy people.

After 1960, the small-scale agricultural model was replaced by large-scale industry and export businesses. This development gave the nation a huge economic boost. The standard of living improved. There were many new material goods, but this prosperity brought new problems.

One problem has been the growing gap between the rich and the poor. Those with better education get higher-paying jobs. Those who can't afford education costs get whatever job they can. Some fall behind during economic growth.

Another problem is urbanization. In the 1970s, about 50% of Koreans lived in urban centers. By the year 2000, the number had risen to 80%.

A third problem is cars. Between 1960 and 1999, the number of registered vehicles in Korea increased from 31,000 to 11,134,000!

From the early 20th century until now, Korea has really changed. It went from one of the poorest to one of the most developed economies. It has also become a very polluted country. Time will tell if Korea can overcome those problems associated with enormous growth.

Memo

Memo